The Golden Dial

THE GOLDEN DIAL

Temporal configuration in
Don Quijote

by

L. A. Murillo

The Dolphin Book Co. Ltd.
Oxford, 1975

PRINTED IN SPAIN

I.S.B.N. 085215-052-0

Depósito Legal: V. 1.790 - 1975   I.S.B.N. 84-399-3728-8

Artes Gráficas Soler, S. A., Valencia

in memoriam

REFUGIO M. MURILLO

CONTENTS

NOTE

The Spanish text of *Don Quijote* is my version of the first editions of 1605, 1615, as prepared for Editorial Castalia, Madrid. The English text is Shelton's translation, 1612-1620 — modernized. London: Gibbings and Co., Ltd., 1895, 4 v., and edited with some minor changes and corrections to conform more accurately with the original.

The Spanish original is quoted alongside the English translation in cases where it has seemed to me both necessary and desirable.

All references to Cervantes' or Shelton's text are given for Part, I or II, and Chapter only.

London, August 1973.

I

INTRODUCTION

N E A R L Y all works of fiction, from the fable and the folk tale to the novel, depend on temporal elements to carry out their plots or to carry forward the actions of their characters. Yet the "timelessness" of the more primitive or less complicated forms of fiction is largely their resistance to any but the slightest differentiation. Primitive myths strike us as timeless precisely because they defy our critical distinctions of past, present, and future, our notions and experience of succession and causation in an irreversible order. The very simplest element is duration, simplest because the least obtrusive. For centuries the art of story telling has been the suspenseful weaving of a fictional duration bearing little or no relation to the consuetudinary lives of listeners. The inobtrusiveness of imaginary duration, one might say, was more or less in degree to the importance one attached to measurable divisions of time within the reality and experience of a given human life time. Men and women everywhere have been conscious of their own life time, its succession and continuity, and inexorable movement toward aging and death. Yet the art of storytelling for centuries provided suspenseful release from just such advertencies. The suspenseful force of such an art, its effect upon us even today, precludes the awareness of an inexorably ordered expenditure of time, in the fiction, the telling of it, or in its reception by the listener. The novel is the most complicated of the forms of modern fiction, and in the novel the sensibilities and consciousness of modern men have found the form that reflects intrinsically their prepossession with the passage of time and its measurement, objective or subjective. [1]

9

Cervantes set his narrative about the Manchegan hidalgo in a time and place according to various literary and poetical conventions regnant at the close of the sixteenth century, and reaching back to such diverse authors as Ariosto and Boccaccio. But *Don Quijote* stands, so to speak, at the continental divide, at the watershed, between the older forms of prose fiction and the hitherside of the modern novel. It is perhaps the first major work of fiction in the western world bringing forth, in opposition to the traditive and fabulous accounts of deeds and intrigues, the imaginative and moral conceptions of character recognizably modern. Its world is the transposition of myth and romance onto a rational cognizance of the processes of everyday experience, with its varieties of shifting and aberrant behavior. The temporality of that world shares with the older forms of fiction, prose or verse, *Amadis of Gaul* or *Orlando furioso,* an almost immutable poetic season and landscape for the lives of its characters, yet its course of successive episodes of an imaginary duration was to yield a circular and archetypal pattern of the process of change and becoming, one followed by countless novelists since the eighteenth century, from Henry Fielding to James Joyce.

The novel came into being as a recognizable literary form in the eighteenth century, for the literatures of the English, French, and Germans. The philosophical, psychological, and mechanical notions of time in that century of "Reason" dedicated to the study of human nature, and in the wake of Newton, Leibnitz, and Locke, would lead novelists to conceive their narratives along the lines of a rationalized sequence of events obeying a formalized temporal verisimilitude. [2] Fielding's *Tom Jones* is probably the best example of a complex plot contrived along the lines of chronological sequence. [3] This regularity had become the convention of neo-classical theorists and critics by 1780, the date of the first effort by Cervantes' commentators to reduce the action of *Don Quijote* to a "chronological plan." The temporal irregularity of plot in *Tristram Shandy* underscores to what extent the principles of a formalized duration and design of temporal antecedent and consequent had become representative of order in the novel of contemporary manners.

After 1800 the sense for an order of time in the novel was vastly expanded to include the whole range of historical and sociological themes, in the wake of the theories of Vico, Kant, and Herder. Temporal duration in the great nineteenth-century novels reveals the variation and multitudinous concerns of novelists engaged in psychological discovery and prepossessed with the idea of social and historical evolution, with likewise an "organic," autonomous, power for the imagination. The ethical value of *Don Quijote* had inspired its eighteenth-century admirers to prescribe a rational order for the extravagances of an episodic action with antecedents in the classical epic. Romantic critical theory, on the other hand, found nothing so essential in it as a unity of design accountable not to explicit and ethical purposes but to implied and esthetic ones. It was now an archetype of romantic, "modern poetry," surpassing the classical "ancient." From its very quality as a "romantic poem" there emerged the evident structure of the archetype capable of depicting the particularities and pluralities of modern life. If a single statement can command so wide a subject, we may say that the comparative relation (for authors, critics, and their readers) that emerged up to 1900 between *Don Quijote* and the great novels of nineteenth-century psychological realism focussed on the autonomous, imaginary world that Cervantes had brought into being, a world unified according to its own artistic laws, from the inner recesses of characters, and their evolving individual identities, to the social and historical horizon that circumscribed it in time and space. The poetic structure of that world would disclose, just beneath the antithesis of its immortal pair, tones and styles at dialectical variance between the parodied and discredited narratives of chivalry and a novelistic form that reabsorbed and transformed them while depicting the life of the senses and the flow of experience. In the eighteenth century, when it became famous as a "comic romance in prose," the real time and course of Don Quijote's adventures were seen as a criticism of the false time and false fictions of the serious and heroic romances. The nineteenth century expressed the same antithesis in terms of illusion and ideality fomented in psychological realism. There came forth thus the twentieth-century view that the nature of this world, and, in principle, of the novel, was a conflict of a new or advanced form imposing its representational techniques over the forms it impugnes and supercedes, a dialectical conflict wherein one kind of novelistic fiction replaces an earlier kind as more genuine. [4] Such a view over so large a body of literature ensures a focus, sooner or later, on the anatomical relation between the episodic structure of mock epic in *Don Quijote* and the epic structure of Joyce's *Ulysses.*

The temporal themes in *Don Quijote* have all the appearances of an inherent factor of its structure, but they have failed to convey any importance to the major critics of Cervantes in this century. Hopefully my study will correct this condition. It was perhaps inevitable that temporal elements should have aroused the interest of Cervantes' critics and commentators in the form of chronology. By 1863, the date of Hartzenbusch's *Diary,* there existed scores of novels since Cervantes with plots drawn along the lines of a unified chronological sequence and duration. Since 1780 nearly a score of efforts to reduce the action of *Don Quijote* to a single chronology by the calendar have left few if any besides their particular propounders convinced. [5] Chronological sequence is indeed an element of time in *Don Quijote,* but it is not the decisive order of temporal elements. An almost total blindness to this on the part of propounders of chronologies, especially since 1940, and a partial blindness on the part of critics, have left a relatively simple problem unclarified. By the same inadequacy the importance of time factors has been distorted, so that where we should have a clear, simple, and meaningful picture, we have a confusion signifying little or nothing.

Yet my concentration on time schemes may invite doubts as to their applicability to a style of narrative introduced long before authors began to think seriously about literary duration and the unity of time for their novels. Our interest in time factors is a contemporary view, from the hitherside of the modern novel. Cervantes' book belongs to the modern world, not only as the unsurpassed archetype of all novels, but for the permanence of the poetical world that surrounds and upholds his cast of characters. Probably no reader or critic today doubts that *Don Quijote* is a novel, in the generic or modern sense. Yet Cervantes never called it a *novela*, though he did use the term for his shorter narratives. He did call it *historia*, but in a mocking sense. He might have been satisfied simply with *libro*. If *Don Quijote* exists for us as a novel, irrespective of our views of what Cervantes intended and accomplished with respect to the state of fiction in 1605 and 1615, then the temporality of its imaginative world exists for us within the outlines of a veritable form. The fact that this form poses critical questions of uneasy magnitude, not the least its definition, has never forestalled our conviction that it exists.

My study is then not an investigation into whether Cervantes could or could not have had any intention, explicit or otherwise, to give his narrative a temporal or chronological unity. Nor is it an attempt to reconstruct such a plan along the lines of subsequent novels. Nor is it a study of time as fictional duration along the lines of studies on twentieth-century novels.

When we describe time elements in *Don Quijote* as "poetical" or "quixotic" we mean we perceive how they relate to the inner logic of its structure. My time schemes and configurations are but a relatively simple attempt to explain and to represent the "quixotic" time of Don Quijote's career in terms mutually acceptable to contemporary readers, literary historians, and critics. The purpose of my study is to lay down the critical basis for dealing with the temporal movement of the entire narrative as it appeared in 1605 and

1615. To do so I have had to investigate to some depth a number of questions buried in the critical commentary on Cervantes. I did not do this for any bibliographical sport, nor as proof of my spade work, but to furnish details of literary history for my total approach. One of the most diverting of the time elements in *Don Quijote* is a result of Cervantes' peculiar frame of mind and style for incorporating the very process of its composition, even its publication, into his narrative. In my third chapter I have hypothesized a time scheme for the composition of the book that clarifies these elements. The time schemes sketched in this introduction are my own device for aligning various materials, textual, historical, bibliographical, into a critical conception. They are the means I hit upon for representing the binary duration of Don Quijote's adventures. This binary movement of narrative events is part of that structure of illusion and fact, fable and reality, that sustains for modern readers the fictive world of Don Quijote and Sancho.

THE GYRES OF SUMMER

In one superb moment of their dialogue, in Chapter 28 of Part II, Don Quijote and Sancho have a heady argument about wages. Sancho, his sore back stiff from effects of the disastrous braying adventure, has threatened to quit his services and return home. The knight, stung by an unsquirely reproach, appears to give in, and tells him to reckon how much is due him, on a monthly basis, as wages. The squire figures up a pay-scale of twenty-four reales monthly, but, in addition, also claims compensation for the unfulfilled promise of an island's governorship at the rate of six reales per month, making thirty reales altogether. The knight is thinking of payment for one, or maybe two months, and agrees.

> —Está muy bien —replicó don Quijote—; y conforme al salario que vos os habéis señalado, veinte y cinco días ha que salimos de nuestro pueblo: contad, Sancho, rata por cantidad, y mirad lo que os debo, y pagaos, como os tengo dicho, de vuestra mano.

—¡Oh, cuerpo de mí! —dijo Sancho—, que va vuestra merced muy errado en esta cuenta; porque en lo de la promesa de la ínsula se ha de contar desde el día que vuestra merced me la prometió hasta la presente hora en que estamos.

—Pues ¿qué tanto ha, Sancho, que os la prometí? —dijo don Quijote.

—Si yo mal no me acuerdo —respondió Sancho—, debe de haber más de veinte años, tres días más a menos.

Diose don Quijote una gran palmada en la frente, y comenzó a reír muy de gana, y dijo:

—Pues no anduve yo en Sierra Morena, ni en todo el discurso de nuestras salidas, sino dos meses apenas, y ¿dices, Sancho, que ha veinte años que te prometí la ínsula? II. 28

—It is very well — said Don Quijote —; and according to the wages that you have allotted unto yourself, it is now twenty-five days since we left our village: reckon, Sancho so much for so much, and see how much is due to you, and pay yourself, as I have bidden you.

—Body of me! — said Sancho — you are clean out of the reckoning; for touching the promise of governing the island, you must reckon from the time you promised til this present.

—Why, how long is it — quoth he — since I promised it?

—If I be not forgetful, said Sancho —, it is now some twenty years, wanting two or three days.

Don Quijote gave himself a good clap on the forehead, and began to laugh heartily, saying:

—Why, my being about Sierra Morena, and our whole travels were in less than two months, and dost thou say it was twenty years I promised thee the island? II. 28

The bemused reader will reflect that this is not the first time a reckoning of wages for the squire gives occasion to a tally of days and months for their story. If nothing so comical as a squire mounted on an ass and demanding payment of wages for his services is conceivable for knighthood, nothing rings so out of place in the style of chivalric romance as an acquittal of it into a bookkeeper's account of calendar days and months. Cervantes was perfectly aware of this delightful absurdity, and perhaps meant to keep to himself just how he had made the most of it.

The knight's disclosure of days and months is linking the action and adventures of the First Part, published in 1605, to the adventures of the Second Part, published ten years later.

Hence one set of impressions we may have about the sequence
of events in the story will come together, linking into one
continuous duration the various episodes up to this point. But
Sancho's claim that a governorship was promised to him not
two months but twenty years ago may well confirm another
set of impressions no less valid. Sancho's memory is not
grappling with external, mathematical calculations of events
and dates, but with illusions and their inner reality. Yet at
the time Cervantes set down the passage in the year 1613 or
1614 it may have struck him as a calculation self-imposed
that indeed something like twenty years had passed since he
had enlisted as squire to Don Quijote, "a neighbouring peasant, a decent fellow," with the fanciful inducement of an
island's governorship that would fall on him almost the next
day. But the chronology of Sancho's employment and earnings
lay now within the book, where his frustrations could welter
in the adventurous course of one or two summers. For the
author, whose literary career had been at the point of extinc-
tion in 1597, as the reign of Philip II closed, those unpaid
wages were a poignant reminder that the sales of the successful First Part had failed to amend his own poverty. Sancho's
expectations were unhappily paralleled by his, and twenty
years of unrewarded hopes were fact and no illusion.

If the reader has formed any definite opinion about the
duration of their narrative from beginning to end, he will
have noted that, in order to agree with Don Quijote that only
two months have passed since the pair set out for the Puerto
Lápice (I.7), he has to overcome an impression not unlike
Sancho's that much more time—narrative time—has elapsed;
so many adventures, so many episodes, dialogues, coming on
thick and fast have surely taken longer. Certainly no *history*
of chivalry was ever confined to the passage of two or three
months. And, moreover, hasn't the First Part of their adventures been published already, and sold, and even translated
abroad? Is the time of their narrative so indefinite that Don
Quijote can be described as entombed in the valedictory verses
to the "history" published in 1605, and then greeted and

celebrated like mythical Amadís in the adventures of the ducal palace that the sequel says took place in 1614? The fact is that as readers we are dealing with two notions of narrative duration woven into the book, and connecting the two Parts.

In the dialogue above the disagreement between knight and squire is not imposed on us as something to be taken seriously. Since the enterprises of both are mock chivalry, and our author's account of them is a fable and a mock history, their calculations have the effect of mock truth exposed and played upon from perspectives of psychical and moral illusion. There exists one calculation of days and months valid for Don Quijote and another valid for Sancho. One feels that the author Cervantes, if ever he considered the matter systematically, kept another. Yet this display of disagreement illuminates as perhaps no other moment in their book an alignment of two planes of narrative sequence. Don Quijote says that nearly three months have elapsed since he and Sancho set out on the sally that began with the attack on the windmills; Sancho's expectations, long frustrated, tell him that was twenty years ago. Yet both overlook the fact recorded in their "history" as published in 1605 that the adventures of windmills-giants, merino sheep-armies, galley slaves, and those in Sierra Morena, took place in August; and here in the sequel, just two days away from arrival at the banks of the Ebro, knight and squire are bound for Zaragoza, where they expect to arrive for the jousts of Saint George, in April. [6]

Readers of *Don Quijote* have overlooked such details for generations, enthralled by the impression that knight and squire, despite changes seemingly of a lifetime undergone, and the passage of weeks and months on the open roads of Spain, appear against a landscape and season that is always summer. For, indeed, just such is the case: the season and its landscape in the First Part is summer, the dog days of July and August. And, although the adventures of the Second Part are immediately consecutive or continuous in an uninterrupted duration, they, too, take place in summer. And by what conception of time and duration can this be? we ask.

Did Cervantes conceive intentionally such a scheme? Or is it a result of his oversights and lapses of memory? Or of imitation, or uninspired convention? For by what recourse to solar movement, poetic or aeroscopic, can the time of a fiction and its seasonal landscape remain arrested or fixed?

Our perplexity is aroused by a binary motion of time interlaced in the sequence and connectives of his episodes, and corresponding to two notions of narrative duration. The first of these notions is a chronological sequence in verisimilar or realistic narrative, where such matters as Sancho's wages must be computed daily or monthly with some accuracy. The second is an imaginative projection of the narrative toward a poetic and indefinite time, where temporal movement may be so imperceptible as to appear suspended indefinitely in a season of perpetual, spring-like summer. The latter pertains to an indefinite and ideal time; indefinite with respect to the historical calendar recording solar movement, and ideal with respect to projected expectations of characters within, and of readers without, the kind of fiction we know as *romance*. In its simplest form this kind of fiction is that realm of "once upon a time" of poetic fancy and wish fulfilment. And this realm is exactly the temporal setting of the chivalric and pastoral romances found in the hidalgo's library by the curate and barber in Chapter 6. These, a verisimilar or realistic (what we shall henceforth call the exemplary) and an ideal and poetic or romantic, are the two temporal movements Cervantes opposed in the initial sally of his First Part, and then, as a consequence of its public success, amalgamated in the time, season, and duration of his Second Part, bringing them together, not without some false starts, into a single, yet binary temporal configuration.

In the dialogue above Don Quijote reckons a duration of time spanning the episodes of the First and the Second Parts computed from the beginning of the second sally and faithful to the course of his narrative from that point. The present day is the "twenty-fifth" of this, the third sally; hence the date, by the calendar, should be a day in October... The first

sally took place in July, and the second followed in August.
An enormous miscalculation is involved if two months or more
later into their narrative knight and squire are engaged in an
episode of a third sally and the season, unchanged, is still
summer. But in point of fact a second order of events and
narrative sequence has been set in motion upon the start of
this third sally. And if these two lines of sequence are linked
to one another, as they undoubtedly are, they are not only
consecutive, that is, the second continues from the first, they
are also in some way synchronous. Yet the hours, days, and
months of Don Quijote's and Sancho's narrative—their actions,
dialogue, aspirations—are inscribed within the sun's movement: diurnal arc and seasonal cycle, within the solar, the
cosmical year. The sequence of their adventures throughout
the First Part and the Second produces the illusion of a lineal
and forward movement from episode to episode, but this
illusion is itself part of their fable. For, in fact, their narrative
is both arrested in time, landscape, and season, and forwarded
in motion; arrested in the seasonal time of a fabled summer,
and motioned in inner, psychical duration and that tangible
succession of events that endows actions, sensations, and
illusions with moral significance.

At the outset of his first sally (I.2), on the plains of Montiel,
the hidalgo invokes a mythical delineation of himself as
knight, out of the past and, for him, historical time of knighthood. But likewise he projects himself and his actions into
a future time of their literary form, knowledge, and acclaim.
The scene is exemplary parody, for his insanity is so peregrine
that he must simulate a mythical role in the style of its
poetical representation. A realistic and exemplary narrative
is projected by design towards its mythical counterpart. The
germ, the nuclear dynamic, of this self-projection is a psychical disorder. But this disorder becomes by its own design
a poetic scheme, self-contained in expectation of its fulfilment:
the *ideal* history of Don Quijote as conceived by an omniscient
mage-historian as yet unnamed. The components of our

configuration are thus projected from the start: an exemplary narrative, a history of chivalry, a mythical orb. The exemplary enacts the fable on the level where the pathological and the moral interact. Thus implicated, the account of chivalry becomes a *mock* history. But the bounds to his characterization, to his fulfilled new self, have been set by the hidalgo-knight, and the horizon with its solar movement that inscribes the merely exemplary time and place of his exploits is mythical, acquiescent to an inner delineation of poetic truth.

> —*Who doubts, in the ensuing ages, when the true history of my famous acts shall come to light, but that the wise man who shall write it, will begin it, when he comes to declare this my first sally so early in the morning, after this manner?* "*Scarce had the ruddy Apollo spread over the face of the vast and spacious earth the golden twists of his beautiful hairs . . . when the famous knight, Don Quijote of the Mancha, abandoning the slothful plumes, did mount upon his renowned horse Rocinante, and began to travel through the ancient and known fields of Montiel*" (*as indeed he did*).
>
> *And following still on with his discourse, he said:*
>
> —*Oh, happy the age and fortunate the time, wherein my famous feats shall be revealed, feats worthy to be graven in brass, carved in marble, and delivered with the most curious art in tables, for a future instruction and memory. And, thou wise enchanter, whosoever thou beest, whom it shall concern to be the chronicler of this peregrine history, I desire thee not to forget my good horse Rocinante . . .*

The force of his chivalry, the dynamic of his insanity, brings into being a mythical figuration of himself the reader will have before him throughout the story of his exploits: the aureole of myth is Don Quijote's by right of wish fulfilment, spurred by interaction of poetry and psychosis.

At its birth, at the time of its genesis in the literary career of its author, the idea and basic plan of *Don Quijote* were those of an exemplary novel; not, strictly speaking, the type of short novel Cervantes published in the collection of 1613, but rather the narrative whose purpose, theme, and style, had emerged in his career as opposed in spirit and execution to the pastoral enterprises of his *Galatea,* published in 1585. William J. Entwistle has pressed this conception of the book to its fullest: "He had reached the zenith of his skill as an exemplary novelist when he sat down to write *Don Quijote,* and what he had in mind to write was, in the first instance, an exemplary novel." [7] The "exemplary" form emerged in the mind of Cervantes when, following a hitherto undisclosed bent, he undertook to explore character and to illuminate it in the full light of contemporary society. Conceived at the lowest point of his fortunes, the seemingly hopeless years 1590-1597, *El ingenioso hidalgo* proved to be the turning point in his career. It marked, however, not only the grandest experiment in exemplary narrative; its idea and plan also described from the first their potential to a surprising extent. From the outset, as we shall see, the initial conception contained the virtual force of its complete unfoldment, even to the year 1615.

The passage on wages quoted above is a moment in the narrative when one line of temporal succession and duration aligns with a second, and where, moreover, these two "chronologies" become coincidental to a third, the chronology of the actual composition of the two Parts. The first line of temporal sequence traces the course and succession of adventures from the beginning of the first sally and illustrates an exemplary duration reaching back into a first summer. The second line traces the course and succession of adventures in the second summer of the sequel. The initial conception (I.2) was to depict Don Quijote against a season and landscape of an unbearably hot day on the plains of La Mancha, in the spirit of parody and mockery of the poetic season and landscape of the romances invoked by him. Yet, in order to maintain that parody whose basis is realistic the duration of the narrative will not exceed the bounds of summer. And Cervantes was to hold to this conception for the "time" of his hidalgo's "history" through the twenty years of its composition. Thus the very element parodied, the indefinite or "poetic" time of chivalric romances, has determined for Cervantes both the temporal limits of his narrative with respect to the calendar and its inner movement with respect to the lives of his characters.

The order of the story that begins in Chapter I of the First Part and according to Don Quijote above had then run for nearly three months, moves forward linking one episode to the next according to Cervantes' exemplary purpose. This narrative sequence of exemplary and prescribed duration begins with the hidalgo's resolve to remake his life after the models of chivalry, and comes to an end when, on his death bed, he regains his sanity and recovers his former self, but in the form of *Alonso Quijano el bueno*. This order of narrative sequence is inscribed within the solar movement of a single year. It moves forward with the passage of time, from episode to episode, according to the cause and pathological delineation of the hidalgo's psychosomatic condition and his character.

The line of narrative sequence that begins with Chapter I of the Second Part of 1615, and according to Don Quijote in the passage above had run for (more than) twenty-five days must be read as consecutive to the first, but in order to read it as continuous through the same summer period its course must be thought of as taking place on another plane. Moreover, the temporal movement of this Second Part renders the adventures of the First immediately anterior to the summer of 1614, without the intervention of ten years or more of the historical calendar. Thus the temporal configuration for the complete work can be illustrated by the motion of two gyres representing each a complete cycle of the solar year, but so aligned that the season of summer for the second may be read as continuous from the close of the summer season of the first. The gyre of the first summer describes the duration and line of sequence of the episodes of the first and second sallies; the gyre of the second summer describes the duration and line of sequence of the third sally.

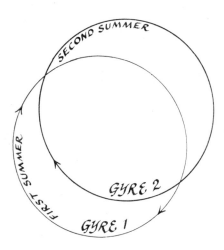

Figure 1

Now, in order to be so aligned the rotation of each gyre must be determined by relation of their respective centers. If the gyre of the first summer revolves around the point representing the time of Cervantes' exemplary narrative ("There lived not long since, in a certain village of La Mancha..." I. 1) the gyre of the second may be thought of as revolving around the center of the mythical year of Don Quijote's adventures, for the "poetic" connective between the narratives of the two Parts is precisely the illusion of Don Quijote as knight-errant and his real identity as an hidalgo of La Mancha. Thus, if the center of revolution for the first summer can be thought of as a fixed date in historical time (1597, as some would have it), its counterpart is a center of a mythical time for his "history" that Don Quijote has projected from the start of his sally. On the fields of Montiel, and according to the parody of an exemplary plan, the gravitational force of psychical energy to and identification with the literary and poetic models of the inspired hidalgo locates, also, the center of his narrative as chivalric romance on the fields of mythical renown.

Will our configuration disclose the meaning of the axial relation between the centers of motion of our gyres? Yes.

THE MYTHICAL HOUR: SUNRISE

There are two moments, two scenes of daybreak in *Don Quijote* of remarkable, strategic importance. The sunrise on the first outing in Part I noted above and, in Part II, the sunrise seen by knight and squire from the shore at Barcelona, on arrival at their final destination. The first signals the beginning of the narrative; the second, its culmination. Cervantes supplied a date for each: a Friday in July for the first, Saint John's Nativity (June 24) for the second. If we draw a line connecting the two centers (points α & β) in our configuration, and extend it in both directions, the points on the two gyres (γ & δ) may be said to be paradigmatic of these two scenes of sunrise.

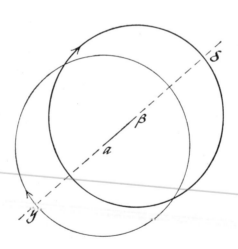

Figure 2

Our configuration shows the scene of the first summer (γ) as the initial moment of the narrative. Setting in motion the adventures of the first sally, it provides the encompassing exemplary focus to a narrative of two summers. Now, on our configuration, the second sunrise (δ) falls at a point on the motion of the second gyre describing not a beginning, but the end of summer. Saint John's Nativity is the feast day of midsummer, and Don Quijote and Sancho arrive at Barcelona after several months of adventures on the road. What manner of anomaly is this? Are we faced with an insuperable obstacle for rendering the chronological inconsistencies of the Second Part into a consistent order? Yes ... insuperable, that is, if we insist on a chronology by the calendar. But temporal movement in *Don Quijote* we have said is binary.

The significance of the first sunrise is the contrast between the overbearing heat on the Manchegan plain the rising sun promises on this day in July ("... the sun did mount so swiftly, and with so great heat, as it was sufficient to melt his brains, if he had had any left" I. 2), and the literary projection of this outing by the knight into a mythical, poetic configuration, with its season, mythological divinities, and landscape. The sunrise Don Quijote describes to himself is poetic myth and a sunrise in spring. [8] His projection of himself as knight-errant defines the orb of myth that encompasses his illusion, just as the Manchegan ground under Rocinante defines the facts of his real identity. Don Quijote invokes a mythical dawn for the inception of his story, and as described by him it is the dawn of the spring equinox. Thus, at this initial moment, there coincide this real or exemplary dawn over the fields of Montiel and the mythical dawn of the year at the spring equinox. On our configuration this would occur when the arc of a circle drawn from point (β) passes through point (γ).

Now, the counterpart of this moment will occur both at point (δ) and where that arc intersects the line of axis at point (ε). The time of Don Quijote's arrival at Barcelona,

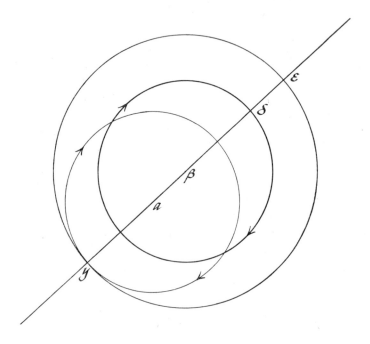

Figure 3

irresrespective of chronology by the calendar, is midsummer, for
that circle drawn from (β) is none other than the orb of myth,
and describes the ideal course of Don Quijote's illusion and
adventures on a mythical summer, announced at the spring
equinox and fulfilled at midsummer. The hour of illusory
fulfilment for Don Quijote at Barcelona aligns the movement
of the second gyre on a mythical orb. The configuration now
shows how the motions of our gyres, if forward according
to narrative sequence and duration, revolve as epicycles
within the sweep of a mythical summer, an orb drawn from
the point of "poetic" time of Don Quijote's projection of
himself on the fields of Montiel as knight-errant.

Has my reader discerned the purpose of my configuration? Is it apparent that a binary movement is involved within the three components of Cervantes' fiction: an exemplary narrative, a history or romance of chivalry, a mythical orb? For now this alignment between points (γ) and (ϵ) becomes decisive for revealing the significance of the festive dawn at Barcelona in Chapter 61 of the Second Part. The city and its populace display the festival air of the annual celebration of midsummer, and, mythically speaking, the solar year points to its plenitude and fulfilment, the summer solstice. Or, rather, the hidalgo's self-figuration as hero-knight is thus emblazoned by analogy to the mythical significance of the solar celebration. It is wish fulfilment, with the reader as accomplice, that invites the annual festivity in Barcelona as acclaim and recognition of the knight Don Quijote, as if in salutation of a solar hero in chivalric armor. Hence the second sunrise, bringing to its moment of plenitude the narrative of the second summer, is also a consummation of a mythical similitude for the first.

The solar "poetic" time of Don Quijote's adventures on the orb of myth is perpetually summer, and swings between the two cardinal points of the spring equinox and summer solstice. The line of axis drawn between them on our dial is thus the alignment for the various scenes of daybreak in Cervantes' story.

Daybreak and dawn descriptions have played traditional roles in poetry and narrative (popular, aristocratic, learned, or courtly) since the remotest times. [9] In Cervantes' episodic order of adventures daybreak signals the close of night, of an interval of sleep, and thus of a new start and new adventure. It is also, and traditionally, a moment of inception, fraught with expectation and promise; hence a moment of linking that renews and establishes narrative tensions. Its consistent and repeated appearance may likewise provide a matter-of-fact count of hours and the passage of night and day. But sunrise is also for its possibilities the most poetic hour of solar time. It provokes, and affiliates, joy and hopefulness to notions of renewal and rebirth. The hidalgo evokes a mythical and youthful Apollo at the outset ("Apenas había el rubicundo Apolo...") as if to signal a regeneration of his middle-aged powers, for the fictional cast he assumes for them, as an impassioned Roland or Amadís, are those of a youth's prowess. The hour of sunrise is thus appropriately the initial moment for his first sally, and likewise for Cervantes the initial point of contrast for the two styles of his narrative, the exemplary, with its supports in realism and verisimilitude, and the mock chivalric and mythical, introduced by way of parody of pastoral romance, and even self parody. [10] The first sunrise and each thereafter described in the course of the narrative will partake of poetic and mythological details as well as the mock or comic details, but the underlying convention in each is that of a mythical dawn in a mythical season. The poetic allusion is invariably to a sunrise over an arcadian landscape of spring grasses and flowers, budding boughs and chirping birds: the dawn of the year, that is, a landscape on the morning of the spring equinox, more suggestive of joy and desire, and expectation in awaitment, than of celestial motion. The season of the world at this mythical hour is appropriately, and by tradition, *primavera*. [11]

If dawn is the mythical hour, then spring, perpetual spring, is the mythical season, and the dawn of the year, the vernal sunrise of any solar year, becomes an enactment of the golden age of myth, when the first races of men lived in a climate and landscape of unending spring. [12] Now, exactly this convergence of myth and poetry provokes the hidalgo's projection of his chivalric role into a future time as wish fulfilment and prophecy. The initial scene of the first outing becomes prophetic by virtue of the mythical past, the golden age Don Quijote dreams of restoring by enacting a new chivalry. Compare the opening phrases of the discourse on the golden age (I. 11) to his psychotic, yet prophetic evocation.

> ¿Quién duda sino que en los venideros tiempos, cuando salga a luz la verdadera historia de mis famosos hechos ...? I. 2

Dichosa edad, y siglo dichoso aquel adonde saldrán a luz las famosas hazañas mías ... I. 2

Dichosa edad, y siglos dichosos aquellos a quien los antiguos pusieron nombre de dorados ... I. 11

Who doubts, in the ensuing ages, when the true history of my famous acts shall come to light ...? I. 2

Oh, happy the age, and fortunate the time wherein my famous feats shall be revealed ... I. 2

Happy time, and fortunate ages *were those whereon our ancestors bestowed the title of golden ... I. 11*

The hidalgo intuits prophetically the future time of his mythical fame in the Second Part. The first sunrise, then, from an exemplary focus, evokes a mythical dawn and projects it toward the future of felicitous fame. On this the first morning of our summer of exemplary narrative the hidalgo's career is projected forward to its consummation. For just as the great dawn of the spring equinox points to and portends, as promise and expectation, the dawn of the summer solstice, so by quixotic decree the summer of exemplary narrative is borne forward onto a mythical time for Don Quijote's adventures, consummated in the scene of arrival at Barcelona in the summer of myth.

My configuration is an attempt to describe in explicit terms the temporal movement of Cervantes' narrative as binary on the planes of exemplary sequence and chivalric myth. As such it is a critical conception, unusual perhaps, and in my mind without mechanical pretensions. Though we may imagine that our gyres describe a course through the twelve months of the calendar and the four seasons of the year, their synchronity as I have drawn it conspires to keep the time of Cervantes' novel an untroubled summer throughout.

PLAN OF THIS BOOK

The following three chapters are designed to complete the outlines of this configuration and are offered more in the way of an exploratory study than as exhaustive or conclusive.

Each chapter retraces the narrative movement of the two Parts from a different angle and with different considerations in mind. They are not intended to be a detailed "textual analysis" of time factors in Cervantes' novel, or of the "time-sense" revealed by him or by his characters. Such a study, in my opinion, can only be attempted on the basis of a thorough search for and definition of the critical concepts to be applied to a book whose time-shape is unprecedented and unmatched in literature. In my "Conclusion" I suggest how my concepts of fictional time can be applied in more comprehensive analyses of temporal themes and structure in *Don Quijote*.

Under the rubric *The Summer of Exemplary Narrative* I review the more notable efforts of commentators and critics to deal with and reduce an essentially binary configuration of narrative time to a single 'verisimilar' and natural sequence. My method is to align this review of historical material with the unfolding of the narrative and likewise with the time schemes laid down in this introduction.

In Chapter Three, I deal with the question of how such external matters as Cervantes' biography and the order of composition of various parts of the book (a somewhat controvertible matter, admittedly) are reflected in, and to what degree were influential in determining, the direction and eventual shape of the book's temporal features. It is here that the fictional life of the book bridges the historical world and actuality of Cervantes' life and the actuality of the story and its characters for Cervantes' readers. The analytical threads of this Chapter, then, align the narrative of his book with historical and biographical considerations.

Under the rubric *The Summer of Myth* I explore, in separate but related sections, the literary antecedents and the elements of the romantic (chivalric) story pattern that, while subordinate to the exemplary and historical in the realistic and verisimilar sense, in effect gathers up and carries them forward in the outward sweep of Don Quijote's mythical summer.

NOTES TO CHAPTER I

1. A review of the question will be found in: A. A. Mendilow, *Time and the Novel* (London: Peter Nevill, 1952, New York: Humanities Press, 1965); Hans Meyerhoff, *Time in Literature* (University of California Press, 1955, 1960); Jean Pouillon, *Temps et roman* (Paris: Gallimard, 1946).

I have depended heavily on the article "Time" in José Ferrater Mora: *Diccionario de filosofía* (Buenos Aires: Editorial Sudamericana, 5th ed., 2 vols., 1965).

The panorama of topics related to physical and historical time may be found in: G. J. Whitrow, *The Natural Philosophy of Time* (London & Edinburgh: Thomas Nelson & Sons, 1961); *What is Time?* (London: Thames and Hudson, 1972); Stephen Toulmin, June Goodfield, *The Discovery of Time* (London: Hutchinson & Co, 1965).

In 1972, as the present study approached completion, the following studies on the European "time-sense" in literature appeared:

Ricardo J. Quiñones, *The Renaissance Discovery of Time* (Harvard Univ. Press, 1972), which does not treat either Spain nor Cervantes, although its concept of the Renaissance is generous enough to include Milton (see p. 501). It suffers from a failure to take into account Glasser's study, published in German in 1936.

Richard Glasser, *Time in French Life and Thought,* trans. C. G. Pearson (Manchester Univ. Press, 1972); in German: *Studien zur Geschichte des französischen Zeitbegriffs* (Munich: Max Hueber, 1936).

2. "If any form for the structure of the novel can be deduced at all from seventeenth and eighteenth century theory, it resolves itself to the progressive narration of consecutive events; this was patterned on the form of the drama in the case of the 'plot-novel', or of the epic in the case of the episodic novel; and it usually adheres to the principles of the beginning, middle and end as defined by Aristotle in his *Poetics.*" Mendilow, pp. 162-163.

3. See Irvin Ehrenpreis, *Fielding: "Tom Jones"* (London: Edward Arnold Ltd, 1964), pp. 16-24; Mendilow, op. cit., "The Revolt of Sterne," pp. 165-197; Theodore Baird, "The Time-Scheme of *Tristram Shandy* and a Source," *PMLA,* 51:803-820 (1936).

4. The following are representative of any number of opinions: Karl Vossler, *Formas poéticas de los pueblos románicos* (Buenos Aires: Editorial Losada, 1959), p. 315; José Ortega y Gasset, *Meditaciones del "Quijote," Obras completas* (Madrid: Revista de Occidente, 1957), vol. 1, p. 384; Eng. trans. by Evelyn Rugg and Diego Marín (New York: W. W. Norton & Co, 1961, p. 139); Harry Levine, "The Example of Cervantes," *Contexts of Criticism* (Harvard Univ. Press, 1958), pp. 79-96.

5. See my Bibliography for a listing of these proposals.

6. This matter is covered in Chapter 4. "Justas de San Jorge" were held three times a year in Zaragoza. My view is that Cervantes most certainly had in mind a spring date.

7. *Cervantes* (Oxford: Clarendon Press, 1967), p. 101.

8. See María Rosa Lida de Malkiel, "El amanecer mitológico en la poesía narrativa española," *Revista de Filología Hispánica,* 8:77-110 (1946); p. 109.

9. See the charming, informative "The 'Origins' of Dawn Poetry," by Arthur T. Hatto, ed., *Eos, an Enquiry into the Theme of Lovers' Meetings and Partings at Dawn in Poetry* (London-The Hague-Paris: Mouton & Co, 1965), pp. 47-68.

10. See Raymond S. Willis, *The Phantom Chapters of the "Quijote"* (New York: Hispanic Institute, 1953), pp. 72-77; Geoffrey Stagg, "La primera salida de Don Quijote: imitación y parodia [por parte de Cervantes] de sí mismo," *Clavileño,* 6, n. 22:4-10 (1953); E. C. Riley, "*El alba bella que las perlas cría*: Dawn Description in the Novels of Cervantes," *Bulletin of Hispanic Studies,* 33: 125-137 (1956).

11. In II. 53 Cervantes mentions five seasons for the year according to the tradition going back to the Middle Ages in Spain, *primavera, verano, estío, otoño, invierno,* quoted on p. 158. Cervantes used only *verano* to describe the season in Don Quijote; see Chap. 2, note 3.

12. A perpetual spring for the first of the four ages of man is largely Ovid's idea, "*ver erat aeternum . . .*" *Meta.,* I. vs. 107. See Wilmon Brewer, *Ovid's "Metamorphoses" in European Culture* (Boston: Cornhill Publ. Co, 1933), pp. 48-52.

II

THE SUMMER OF EXEMPLARY NARRATIVE

OUR single, yet binary configuration of time implies not only that two planes of duration and narrative sequence are involved, but that the bounds of the first summer period encompass the second, while the second summer will also inscribe the first. Further, something even more surprising occurs in *Don Quijote*: the binary configuration derives from the versions of the story told by two different authors, each subscribing to a particular method and form of narrative.

The anonymous — and *second* — author who begins the story has an exemplary purpose. He proceeds to tell it much like the author of *Novelas ejemplares,* and it is cardinal in his exemplary design that he begin with and narrate throughout only the essentials. He is narrating an exemplary story about a self-transformation, not a biography. Therefore, he excludes all references to years and events in the hidalgo's lifetime prior to his transformation. Whether we understand his initial disclosures to be a conscious rejection and parody of the biographical chivalric chronicle or of the autobiographical picaresque tale, or that they are an assertion of his right to place his character in a situation of complete autonomy, is a purely secondary matter. Of greater importance is the disclosure of the causes — social, literary, psychological, of the aberration that provokes his metamorphosis into Don Quijote, because these causes underline the exemplary course of cause and effect in his story. This narrator, in many respects, can be thought to be without antecedents in literary history.

The Arab historian Cide Hamete introduced in Chapter 9 as the author of a supposed original has more clearly defined antecedents. He derives largely from the amalgamation of elements from the medieval chronicle into the prose form of chivalric romance (thirteenth century and later). It is from the form of a medieval chronicle, or its parody, that so many of the time disclosures in *Don Quijote* are derived, a circumstance that has led to inevitable confusion in the minds of those who would see in them evidence of a perfectly verisimilar chronology. The form of a feudal chronicle accounted for the complete sequence and duration of events in the life span of royal or noble individuals and dynasties. But at the time that the substance of chivalric romance — essentially poetic — was recast into prose form the distinctions between history and romance were never carefully drawn. Their outlines were not only blurred, they were merged, and had been for centuries. The storytellers of romance assumed an historical frame for an account of chivalric adventures because they expected, in part, to gain credibility for stories that were essentially legendary and marvellous. If at the inception of the story our hero's delineation is a consequence of his autonomy in an exemplary account, at its close his autonomy will have become a consequence of the historical time (1610-14) in which his final exploits take place. That he assumes an historical actuality as his story approaches its consummation is the final consequence of Cervantes' inversion through parody of the pseudo-historical framework to a chivalric romance.

When Cervantes introduces Cide Hamete at a strategic moment, he is only completing the idea already disclosed in Don Quijote's conceit about the sage historian who would chronicle his exploits. The supposedly original version — whether the work of Cide Hamete or previous to him — would presumably narrate his adventures in the form of a 'history,' but its essence would be nearly the opposite of a verisimilar chronicle. Its essence would be romantic, and its temporal movement determined by magical and mythical attributes. From the moment Don Quijote calls into being the sage historian of his exploits, the story just under way has proliferated into the Quixotic fiction, that is, a fiction

within fiction, each with its corresponding temporal movement.

Though presumably subordinate, or *second,* to the historian, the anonymous narrator has determined a diurnal scale
and tempo to the first two outings according to his exemplary
plan and purpose. His method is nearly clinical. He begins
by disclosing the hidalgo's social and personal characteristics,
then goes on to detail his physiological attributes and discloses
how they supplement his "humor" or temperament. The in-
ordinate passion for reading books of knight-errantry is as
much a consequence of the hidalgo's social isolation as of
his psychosomatic condition, but, in turn, this excessive reading produces certain physiological and psychological effects.

> *... he plunged himself so deeply in his reading of these books, as*
> *he spent many times in the lecture of them whole days and nights;*
> *and in the end, through his little sleep and much reading, his*
> *brains dried up, in such sort as he lost wholly his judgment. I. 1*

Likewise, he suggests the affinity between the fantasies contained in those books and the delineation of their heroes, and
the fact that the hidalgo is choleric, *ingenioso,* and has spells
of melancholy. All this is preliminary to tracing the day-to-
day course of his psychosomatic behavior.

The initial period of his second outing, beginning with
the attack on the windmills, is an outpouring of choleric
temperament (Chs. 8-19), thereon he lapses into a melancholy
state (Chs. 22-31), and is brought home for rest. The possible
remedy and cure for the mental and physical excesses the
hidalgo will undergo are not so much described as prescribed:
food, rest, and prolonged sleep. At the close of each of his
three outings, on returning home, he goes to bed after a
curative meal, and falls into deep, restorative sleep. "... within
two days after, Don Quijote got up, and the first thing he
did was to go and visit his books ..." (I. 7). "*Fifteen days*
he remained quietly at home, without giving any argument
or seconding his former vanities ..." (I. 7). His fantasies will
be played out in the course of a few weeks, while undergoing

experiences that exacerbate and thus exhaust a temperament oscillating between states of rage (the mock battle with the biscayan) and depression and melancholy (penance in the wilds of Sierra Morena). The exemplary design behind these 'clinical' disclosures is so intricate that only inspired scholarly analysis coupled with great imagination can do justice to it. [1]

The hidalgo's irrational behavior is thus a psychosomatic complex whose symptoms this second author is prepared to unfold on the scale of their diurnal and even hourly issuance. He sees his subject on the scale of the natural, the physiological delineation of his hero's psychosis. His story takes place in summer and begins on a torrid day in July because the excessive heat has exacerbated the psychosomatic tendencies of the Manchegan hidalgo. The heat of the weather has quickened the consequences of the "drying up" of his brains, and he ventures forth alone in July in search of adventures when neither the weather, nor the fall and rise of the temperature, will encumber his free movement about the countryside by day or night. This is the basis of the verisimilitude intended in the comment about the effect of the sun's heat on his brains and the contrast it provokes with the apostrophic projection of himself.

Now the "earlier" and supposedly "original" version of these two outings would depict that same course of events as genuine adventure in the style of a chivalric history. There, however, they would not be depicted as a whole, but as a segment of a complete history, and without the definitive beginning and close that the second author has imposed on them. In this version, the duration of the adventures in the first two sallies would be all-but indefinite, and suspended in the time of a fabled summer.

Their narrative time is a season of high or full summer, the dog days of July and August, in accordance with an exemplary plan and design that follow certain traditional beliefs expressed in poetry and folklore. [2] This is the season of "*aestas*," *estío*, but this particular term is never applied. Cervantes apparently preferred to substitute it with *verano*, the term used to describe the season throughout Part II. *Verano*, in the sixteenth century, was normally applied to the season of late spring up to midsummer (May and June), but also to what we would call spring (April through June), because *primavera* (March) was used in the more exact sense of "beginning of summer." [3] If the requirements of the story in Part I call for a limited duration, in accordance with the exemplary plan, the requirements of Part II call for a more or less indefinite duration in which the season of *verano* becomes so prolonged that it actually recurs. The structure of *Don Quijote* is one of fiction within fiction, but these so equilibrated that from the center of each the whole may be seen as a configuration of either fiction — either an exemplary story or a mythical "history." Hence the temporal unfolding of the story will be a process in which the spatial requirements of an account of chivalry — the distances covered by the free-moving protagonist — are delimited by the temporal requirements of an exemplary story.

The narrative of the first day assumes a temporal frame, the passing of the hours from dawn to dusk: "Casi todo aquel día caminó sin acontecerle cosa que de contar fuese, de lo cual se desesperaba..." (I. 2). The hidalgo despairs because for an entire day nothing worthy of retelling happens to him. The day has apparently gone by purely as a unit of duration or an interval. As a chivalric venture it is strictly a minus, a negative event and a negative disclosure. [4] At nightfall he comes to an inn; thereon follow the evening meal, the comical vigil of arms, and the dubbing scene with innkeeper and the two damsels. These scenes, and those of the second day, provide the most vivid satirical exposure of the hidalgo's enterprise; they also expose the limitations that confined Cervantes as long as the literary form of a chivalric "history" remained only a figment of the hidalgo's fantasy and not an integral element of a parodic style merging fictions. Yet this initial phase of his techniques of satire and parody has determined the movement of the entire exemplary story.

The subsequent inscribing of one fiction by another will proceed on the coincidence between the unit of exemplary duration — the day — and the unit of narrative movement — the episode. The account of the second day is wholly taken up by two episodes, the rescue of Andrés and the adventure of silk merchants travelling to Murcia. The narrative moves forward with solar motion, two days and their nights. This is exemplary duration, and the account of events in episodic form is adjusted accordingly, their beginning, climax, and outcome fixed strategically within the sun's course, and, as in the vigil of arms at the inn, the moon's position.

We have the character's lifetime and two days duration under exemplary exposure. Yet, by virtue of a parody that will take its cue from the psychosis of the hidalgo, we can conceive these two days re-enacted as if their episodes were dislodged fragments of some vast chronicle, hoary with age, alluding to a magnificent scale of chivalric achievement, where the hero is nearly as perfect in epic virtue as the literary form in depicting it. That "history" would obey solar movement to perfection, configure nothing less than a mythical expression for knighthood, and transfigure our hidalgo into nothing less than a solar hero.

HISTORICAL PERSPECTIVE

When accounted for episode by episode, nearly all time references in *Don Quijote* have an air of improvisation. By this I mean that their role in the narrative seems at first glance random, like so many other features. The narrative is a constant flow of situations and events, mishaps and surprises. Experience is drawn problematical. The course of nature runs constant, yet its effect on human lives is ever-changing, apparently fortuitous and incidental. That the day Don Quijote sets out on his first sally is a day in July, that the moon shines full that night, are in themselves, and for most readers, expendable disclosures; combined or emphasized they acquire the fixity that such details impose on lives observant of the calendar, the weather, and the clock. But as each detail

appeared in the narrative it came forth fortuitous, and only
when we caught the exemplary effect intended did we feel
it occasioned:

> Y así, ... sin que nadie le viese, una mañana, antes del día,
> que era uno de los calurosos del mes de julio ... salió al campo.
> I. 2
> A dicha, acertó a ser viernes aquel día ... I. 2
> Acabó de cerrar la noche; pero con tanta claridad de la luna,
> que podía competir con el que se la prestaba ... I. 3
> La del alba sería ... I. 4

Now, of course the days and nights of Alonso Quijano
have happened in units of twenty-four hours; of course the
distances he travels over the plains of La Mancha are measurable in terms of a map, compass, and a timer. But precision
in these matters is hardly necessary except in isolated moments of his narrative. As an exemplary account it pays
homage to the inexorability of natural forces on his character,
like the heat of July, or the calendric order of days and dates.
To the neoclassical interpreters of his story we owe the earliest notions about its uniformity. Taking those time references
as evidence exclusively of a chronological sequence and a
'natural' order of events following the calendar, the early
analysts would assume that the book's entire order of episodes
obeyed (or disobeyed) the principle of regularity and mathematical measurement. The episode of the fulling hammers,
or the puppet-play, were drawn in detail to a scale nearly
life-like. The life and deeds of Alonso Quijano and Sancho
Panza moved before the observer with veritable, and verifi-
able, mathematical clarity, their temporal outlines the order
of social existence moulded by the inexorable exigencies of
nature. The pace was the non-exceptional: dawn to dusk,
nightfall to daylight, the diurnal rhythm of an everyday life.
Cervantes did conceive a solar and diurnal rhythm and scale
for the lives of his characters, but he could not have been
concerned with their uniformity and measurement.

He had of course a feeling for the passage and motion
of time and its effects on individuals and customs. The very

words *tiempo, hora* appear repeatedly in *Don Quijote* with
a variety of personal and traditional meanings,[5] and bring into
play the formulas of chivalric authors. References throughout
are made to the hour of the day and night with regularity,
but the only instrument for measuring, not time, strictly
speaking, but solar motion is the astrolabe (II. 29). It can be
said that Cervantes had certain views on the natural creation
amounting to "ideas" about human and physical nature. The
same may be said about his views on the historical past.
But one cannot say that his suppositions about duration and
solar time amounted to an "idea," a conceptualization based
on sensation, measurement, and consciousness of temporal
motion. His cosmography was hispano-christian, theocentric
and ptolemaic.

Conceptualizations and theories — that is, ideas — about
time and temporal duration arise from either a prolonged
awareness of its passage or a systemized measurement of
it, or a combination of these. Cervantes' age is notable for
the literary expression it gave to the awareness of the brevity
of individual existence within temporal motion. The theme in
Góngora and Quevedo is monumental.[6] But we have no
evidence to suppose that temporal awareness for him or for
the greater number of his contemporaries was based on
prolonged familiarity with the instruments for measuring
time, even sand clocks or candles. It is needful to recall that
the measurement of time in 1600, and the rationalist conception of its passage were rudimentary by the standards of
even 1700. The great theories and speculations about physical
time and space and their mechanical measurement belong
to the seventeenth-century scientific revolution: Galileo, Des-
cartes, Newton. In Cervantes' day there were public and
domestic mechanical clocks with their chimes and a few
personal time pieces, such as the portable sun dial. And life
ordered according to the rule of monastic institutions and
churches with their customs for marking the hours and festivals went on as it had for centuries, with little need for
change or improvements.

The regularity of solar or physical time in units of hours and seconds did not become familiar to the population of Europe until well into the eighteenth century. And until then a scientific and uniform measurement of time could not instruct or intervene in the consciousness of men and women as order or precision in their daily lives. One thinks of Kant in his later life, setting out for his daily afternoon walk precisely at four, so regularly that his neighbors set their watches by his appearance at the door of his house. The notion that the passage of time was absolute and uniform is a rationalist accompaniant of the widespread theories in the eighteenth century about a universal human nature uniform for all races and periods. Yet the investigation into the historical past and social institutions was to reveal variety, change, and evolution, so that the time-sense, both subjectively and historically, among Europeans was to be radically altered by 1800.

The temporality of *Don Quijote* is indeed an innovation in fiction, but only partially for the rationalist and exemplary scale it provides for its characters. Don Quijote believes he enacts in his new life a new knighthood, and that, like Amadís', his deeds belong to the timeless realm of literary heroes. His illusion is "quixotic," but so are the narrative movement and styles of his book. For Don Quijote, his deeds, his adventures, are depicted in the time of their essence as poetry. And they are so to almost any reader who identifies with his illusion. Yet because in this movement the immediate scale is necessarily the verisimilar and natural day-by-day account it had an irresistible attraction for certain readers in the eighteenth century who recognized in it the episodic art of the epic rendered into a natural and rational movement of narrative duration. As such it would be uniform, and its verisimilitude commensurate with the calendar and the almanac. The starting point for that uniformity would be, of course, an historical date for the first outing. In 1737 Gregorio Mayáns y Siscar observed: "Whoever wou'd take the pains to form a Diary of *Don Quixote*'s Sallies, will find *Cervantes'*

Account pretty erroneous, and not conformable to the Accidents and Adventures related." [7] He had deduced that the "natural" verisimilitude of an order of days, months, and years was at variance with the hero's picture of himself. [8] Yet, by default, the premise had been laid down: a diary — or chronology — could be extracted from the book and assigned to an historical date. Vicente de los Ríos set his course between this premise and another: a day-to-day accounting for the action in the course of the twelve months of the year will give the "natural" duration of Cervantes' story.

PLAN CRONOLÓGICO: 1780

Vicente Diego Gutiérrez de los Ríos (1732-1779) was an artillery officer by profession and a biographer and critic of Cervantes by literary avocation. It is the artillery theorist one is likely to think of on looking through his "Chronological Plan." [9] He was easily the most earnest of Cervantes' neoclassical critics, and he drew the disapproval of even his fellow critics for the audacity of detail in comparing *Don Quijote* to the *Iliad* and *Aeneid*. At the center of this comparison is the idea of an epical unity of action contained within a duration of days. His Plan was taken up and disputed almost point by point by the commentator Diego Clemencín who branded it an ill-spent effort, [10] and Cervantists have followed suit without lingering to look at its import. It is pointless to disparage it, or to dismiss it as a hopeless enterprise. Nor is it simply an historical curiosity in Cervantean criticism. Ríos applied a single line of interpretation to the various details about duration and intervals and drew conclusions that countless readers to this day have guessed at without knowing what they were looking for. Ríos was the first to make explicit what he and other eighteenth-century admirers conceived to be the grand, epical outlines of Cervantes' "fable," the unity of its action contemplated as a temporal duration. We are in a position to see that what he discovered was Cervantes' innovation in rendering the loose time factors of an epic onto the scale of a verisimilar, natural, fable, by extending the Aristotelian concept of the unity of time to cover an actual expenditure of measurable time factors. In other words, what Ríos plotted was a time plan for the exemplary course of Don Quijote's adventures: a chronology for the exemplary narrative, on the scale of its day-to-day natural sequence. Now, in order to arrive at this Ríos had perforce to adumbrate a major structural condition, and in a way that only twentieth-century criticism was to make permanently feasible.

The idea that the order of episodes in *Don Quijote* is not a primary factor in the story, and that they could be shifted or re-ordered in almost any sequence, has been a favorite one of readers and critics, who perhaps conceive that its keynote lies in the serial or intercalative mode, or in some more elevated art such as "Humor," and have never looked for or intuited a unified design. Ríos contemplated the grand scale of Cervantes' episodic order and narrative movement and lay hold of the single line of cause and effect across the intercalated tales and episodes and linking them all into a single verisimilar plot. Moreover, he grasped that the "magnitude" of their unity was the depictment of Don Quijote's insanity carried forth to its exemplary ending. In his own way he perceived that the psychological delineation of the hero as a narrative process prescribed the unity of succession and duration according to a natural verisimilitude.

After, Don Quijote liberated the galley slaves (I. 22),

he and Sancho entered the Sierra Morena, where they passed the night [i.e., according to Cuesta's 2nd. ed.]. The following day, they found the portmanteau, and met Cardenio on the same mountain. On the twenty-sixth [day of the action, by Ríos' calculation], after the quarrel with Cardenio, Don Quijote determined to remain and do penance, while he sent Sancho with the letter to Dulcinea, and the order for delivering the three ass-colts. This order was dated 22d of August in that year. Hence it may be inferred, as this was the twenty-sixth day since Don Quijote's first sally, that he first left his house on the 28th of July. On the following day, namely, the 23d of August, and the twenty-seventh of the action, at midday, Sancho arrived at the inn, where he met the Curate and the Barber, who made him turn back to seek his master (I. 23-32). [11]

Ríos, then, isolated and extracted what we have called the first line of narrative sequence. His miscalculation, and it would be a major one as we shall see, was to discount, indeed, to refute, all evidence of 'the second line of narrative sequence, thereby providing a Plan that explained the duration of the action as an interval of "one hundred and sixty-five days," from July to January.

Ríos traced the course of adventure and episode for the summer of exemplary narrative, that is, for the summer of the initial conception. That course would assume the episodes of the Second Part to be contiguous by the calendar, and thus to take place in the fall and winter months, from September to January. Ríos summed up his calculations as follows:

REVIEW OF THE PLAN AND DURATION OF THE WHOLE FABLE

As Cervantes supposes his hero to be a modern one, and Don Quijote himself continually alludes to recent events, we must conclude him cotemporary with Cervantes. And the First Part of the *Quijote* having been published in 1605, his first sally may be supposed to have happened in 1604. Upon this supposition the following computation is founded:

	Days	[Total duration]
Don Quijote first sallies forth on the 28th July, and returns on the 29th, 1604.	2	
He remains at home 18 days	18	[20]
He goes forth a second time on the 17th August, and returns on the 2nd September	17	[37]
He remains in his house 31 days ...	31	[68]
A third time he sallies forth, on the 3rd October, at night, and returns on 29th December	87	[155]
He is confined by illness from the 30th December 1604, till the 8th January 1605, on which day he died.	10	[165]
Total	165	

Or 5 months and 12 days.

A SUMMER'S TALE

The principle applied by Ríos is that the passage of fictional time is uniform by a "natural" computation based on the calendar, the clock, and the almanac. Don Quijote's first sally, a matter of two days, takes place at the close of July, and after eighteen days the second sally continues for a span of two weeks through August into September. Then, after a month's interval, the third sally begins in October and continues into November, December, and January. Now Ríos recognized that the consistency between the First and Second Parts was a summer setting,[12] but once having computed a chronological sequence for the First, his very conception of a verisimilar duration, so rationalist was it, obstructed his applying any but the idea of a chronological connective into the Second. Thus Cervantes, either because of haste or carelessness ("... Cervantes wrote in haste and never corrected or revised what he wrote ..."), had been led into a series of miscomputations. Ríos would furnish the corrective, according to the rule of uniformity in temporal passage by the calendar. His audacity was nearly foolish, for he all-but-premised that the unity of action depended on a uniformity of chronological succession.

> The enchantment of Dulcinea took place on the 6th of October, after which Don Quijote and Sancho journeyed towards Saragossa. On the close of this day they met the players, who said they had performed the piece called "Parliament of Death" that morning, which was the octave of Corpus Christi. Cervantes is here guilty of an error in chronology, by making the octave of Corpus Christi happen in October. He is equally wrong in his geography, by saying that Don Quijote and Sancho, after leaving Toboso, took the road to Saragossa; because every adventure that happened to Don Quijote after this, till he arrived at the lakes of Ruydera, took place on the south of Toboso, while Saragossa is in quite a contrary direction.

Ríos censured and corrected one by one the "errors" in chronological interval and distances. When, in II. 28, Don Quijote says that "it is now twenty-five days since we left our village" he is mistaken, because by a "correct" count it is "only seventeen days."

> Two days after, that is, on the 22nd of October, Don Quijote arrived at the Ebro, where he met with the adventure of the enchanted bark. Cervantes is here guilty of a great geographical error. The distance from the inn, where the puppet-show was, to the river Ebro..., divided into five days journey, [would make] fourteen leagues for Rocinante to travel in each day; a thing impossible either for him, or Sancho's Dapple.

Cervantes' anachronisms with regard to the season are only exceeded by those he commits when he sets down certain dates.

> The following day, after dinner, was the adventure of Trifaldi, and at night that of Clavileño, or the flying horse. Sancho also now wrote a letter to his wife Teresa, dated 20th July 1614. This is a palpable anachronism, according to the chronology established by Cervantes in the first part; it was, in fact, the 30th of October; and as that part was printed in 1605, the date ought, at least, to have been as early as 1604, to make it all probable.

Yet the other side of the principle applied by Ríos is that Cervantes had conceived the action of his story according to the unity of character depictment, with its unities of time and place, and in this he was not wrong. He discovered the inner artistic sense of each one of those disclosures about the passage of time, perceived that they pointed to a radical mode of narrative, that Cervantes was not merely interjecting them in a parodic way, but tracing a temporal design, a purposeful plan.

Ríos believed he was apotheosizing the epic scale of Cervantes' fable by drawing its temporal lines of a natural verisimilitude according to his conception of the *Iliad*. He was overzealous in his computation because he believed he had struck the great artistic relation between Cervantes and Homer. Yet to read through his Plan is to watch Cervantes' story contract before our eyes into the epitome of a rationalist fable with a time scheme, a kind of science fiction of neoclassicism. But it is really more interesting for the paradox that both sustains and, as it were, betrays it.

On the one hand Ríos drew out and emphasized the epical scale of a masterpiece of realistic and verisimilar art. On the other hand he discounted the very element of parody that is for us the surest, the stylistic and structural relation to the epic mode. Ríos had not far to go in the literature of his century to find the satire of mock-heroic and romance applied to everyday details. The conventions of narrative whereby the summer season is the time and setting for romance were even more familiar to him than they are to us. In 1773 Richard Graves had published *The Spiritual Quixote,* a comic romance with the subtitle *or the summer's ramble of Mr. Geoffry Wildgoose.* It must have been then but a peculiarity of temperament that made him so sensitive to Cervantes' vein of ridicule that he would discount any but a didactic import in it. He took Cervantes at his word with respect to the fictional and fabulous world of the romances of chivalry. Cervantes had meant to discredit their falsities of time, place, and character, using ridicule and satire to reduce their fanciful attributes to a truthful fable. When he ridicules their poetic scenes of lovemaking, or battles, or dawn descriptions, against his real or lifelike scale, our reaction should be to complete that attack on their false poetry by penetrating to this true sense of his exemplary fact and event, discredit those facetious elements he parodies, along with the false omniscience of Cide Hamete, and to discount their intervention in a verisimilar fable.

This reaction would be calculated, indeed even computed, to eclipse and dispel any view of that roseate horizon of myth and romance that brightens Don Quijote's career. And so it is that the neoclassical Ríos failed to identify the prototype of mythical hero in Don Quijote behind the mock-heroic artifice. A wondrous paradox. For Ríos the great arc of Don Quijote's trajectory in the Second Part, with its sustained advance into the future of his felicitous fame, was but a succession of admirable wayfare exposures running through the months of October, November, and December. Thus he actually computed a "natural" course for the hidalgo's adventures counter to Cervantes', a solar movement in decline through fall and winter.

For Ríos the sun never rose over the horizon of the summer of myth. The festival of Corpus Christi, the ducal hunt and Merlin's prophecy, even the dates of letters, July 14, 1614, and August 16, were infractions in chronology. Inconceivable that as a parody of chivalry the sunrise over Barcelona should be at midsummer, for by the calendar the day should be the 30th of November. Yet the notion that Cervantes was careful to emphasize, consistently, details about the summer weather in order to keep the mock adventures of chivalry plausible never occurred to him.

> ... presto se les pasó el día y se les vino la noche, y no tan clara ni tan sesga como la sazón del tiempo pedía, que era en la mitad del verano. II. 34
> ... and the day was soon past, and the night came on, and not so light and calm as the time of the year required, it being about midsummer ...

On the way back from Barataria Sancho falls into a pit in the darkness of night.

> ... le tomó la noche, algo escura y cerrada; pero como era verano, no le dio mucha pesadumbre ... II. 55
> ... the night took him, somewhat dark and close; but being summertime, it troubled him not much ...
>
> ... llegaron a su playa la víspera de San Juan en la noche ... II. 61
> ... they arrived on the beach at Barcelona during the night of Saint John's Eve ...

That the season of the year should remain summer throughout the Second Part is not only a palpable, though quixotic, absurdity, it is also a necessity. For, by Ríos' own rule of verisimilitude the weather and landscape, during the months of October, November, and December, in the provinces of La Mancha, Aragón, and Cataluña, are all but impossible as the scene and place of adventures under the open skies, exposed to the winds and inclemencies.

By the kind of fortuitous paradox that enables a literary masterpiece to recreate itself in a reader's sensations, Ríos' proposal found accord where least expected. How many readers, following the declining course of Don Quijote's fortunes, from the ducal palace to the sands at Barcelona, have felt the scene and season more commensurate with fall and winter than midsummer? Ríos fixed the day of Don Quijote's entry into Barcelona as November 30; the day of defeat on December 6; his joyless journey back to the village from December 18 to 29; his death on January 8. How many of our dear nineteenth-century readers, in the saddest book ever written, have intuited this wintry course for their hero? At least one expressed his intuition with complete affinity. The lovely passage from Heinrich Heine's *Reisebilder,* in a winter of disenchantment, found more than a few to share his feelings. One year, not far into the nineteenth century, he tells us, his delight was to read *Don Quijote* as a boy, from beginning to end, in Tieck's translation. He began the first chapters in May . . .

> It was a beautiful day, the blooming spring lay basking in the silent morning light, listening to the compliments of that sweet flatterer, the nightingale, who sang so softly and caressingly, with such a melting fervour, that even the shyest of buds burst into blossom, and the lusty grasses and the fragrant sunshine kissed more rapturously, and the trees and flowers trembled from very ecstasy. But I seated myself on an old mosscovered stone bench . . . not far from the water-fall, and feasted my little heart with the thrilling adventures of the valiant knight. In my childish simplicity I took everything in sober earnest; no matter how ridiculous the mishaps visited upon the poor hero by fate, I thought it must be just so, and imagined that to be laughed at was as much a part of heroism as to be wounded; and the former vexed me just as sorely as the latter grieved my heart. I was a child, and knew nothing of the irony God has interwoven into the world . . . and I wept most bitterly, when, for all his chivalry and generosity, the noble knight

gained only ingratitude and cudgels. As I was unpracticed in reading, I spoke every word aloud, and so the birds and the trees, the brooks and the flowers, could hear all I read, and as these innocent beings know as little as children of the irony of the world, they, too, took it all for sober earnest, and wept with me over the sorrows of the unfortunate knight.... Dulcinea's knight rose ever higher in my esteem, and my love for him grew stronger and stronger the longer I read in that wonderful book, ... so that when autumn came I had reached the end of the story, — and I shall never forget the day when I read the sorrowful combat wherein the knight came to so ignominious an end.

It was a gloomy day; dismal clouds swept over a leaden sky, the yellow leaves fell sorrowfully from the trees, heavy tear-drops hung on the last flowers that drooped down in a sad faded way their dying little heads, the nightingales had long since died away, from every side the image of transitoriness stared at me — and my heart was ready to break as I read how the noble knight lay on the ground, stunned and bruised, and through his closed visor said, in tones faint and feeble, as if he was speaking from the grave, "Dulcinea is the fairest lady in the world..."

That was long ago. Many new springs have bloomed forth since then, yet their mightiest charm has always been wanting, for, alas! I no longer believe the sweet deceits of the nightingale, spring's flatterer; I know how soon his magnificence fades, and when I look at the youngest rosebuds I see them in spirit bloom to a sorrowful red, grow pale, and be scattered by the winds. Everywhere I see a disguised winter. [13]

THE MYTHICAL SPRING OF ALONSO QUIJANO

Cide Hamete Benengeli tells us in the Second Part of this History, and Don Quijote his third sally, that the vicar and barber were almost a whole month without seeing him, because they would not renew and bring to his remembrance things done and past. Notwithstanding, they forbore not to visit his niece and the old woman, charging them they should be careful to cherish him, and to give him comforting meats to eat, good for his heart and brain, from whence in likelihood all his ill proceeded. II. 1

The thread of our exemplary narrative continues intact into the sequel of 1615. [14] Only a month has gone by since the return to the village: the characters reappear; their age, habits, whims, illusions, unchanged. And the scene is the hidalgo's bedchamber, for the close of a month's interval signals the end of the convalescent period. The same bedchamber, at the close of the sequel, is the scene of the final moments and death of Alonso Quijano.

No sooner the sequel gets underway than we discover, however, new terms for the connective back into the episodes of the First Part. Those episodes are not only the recent, immediate past, they are that past preserved within literary form. Not just because Cervantes wished to have his characters reply to those critics who had found his efforts defective, but because the First Part was now, at the time the opening chapters were written (1609-1611), [15] a published book, a literary reality, and had replaced the romances of chivalry as a basis of contrast and criticism. For the characters, as for the author, the experiences recorded in that published history concede to the present scene and time the finality of an acquired literary form. In the First Part the elements of literary chivalry could intrude into the exemplary account only as an unabashed parody. Knight and squire performed adventures as yet comparable to none, for they were unlike any to be found in the genuine romances. Now the published form of the First Part intercedes as the point of departure for a series of new experiences.

The interval of one month, as a connective, explains that the action will continue, from the close of the First Part, through the same season, thus sustaining the fictional thread across the interval of historical time of several years. But in order to continue from that point the hero's delineation is to be sustained throughout an action that begins anew, in the course of spring to summer. In this way the hero's poetic illusion of himself and the natural course of time coincide. That is, the psychosomatic delineation of Don Quijote is now magnified onto a mythical scale.

In the First Part Don Quijote's fame as a knight is a psychosis played out to deception; in the Second his fame has become the reality of Cervantes' world and public, and whether bequeathed by him or by a sardonic or admiring public, that fame confirms the illusions and nourishes the ambitions of the hidalgo. Cervantes had perforce to embody these in a new character, created, as it were, out of unprecedented materials. Sansón Carrasco is therefore the harbinger, and subsequently the antagonist, of Don Quijote's mythical trajectory in the sequel.

> *Don Quijote was monstrous pensative, expecting the bachelor Carrasco, from whom he hoped to hear the news of himself in print, as Sancho had told him; and he could not be persuaded that there was such a history, since yet the blood of enemies killed by him was scarce dry upon his sword-blade, and would they have his noble acts of chivalry already in the press? II. 3*

How subtle the replacement of the defamed romances by the intruder, this fanciful *history* of events just past. The span of one month preserves the unities of time, place, and character, but Cervantes intuited them on the level of his parody. According to Ríos' calendar the month should be September; according to the demands of parody and the mythical delineation of Cervantes' hero that month is an unspecified interval that allows the action of the Second Part to move forward to another spring and summer, without an intervening winter. And, again, Sansón Carrasco is the exponent of an incentive and goal for the knight, who apparently is without design or even motive for a third sally.

The First Part concluded with the disclosure of a forthcoming third sally whose destination was Zaragoza: "... only fame hath left in the memories of The Mancha, that Don Quijote after his third escape was at Zaragoza, and present at certain famous jousts made in that city ..." I. 52. Notably, already in 1604 the knight's fame and jousts at Zaragoza were coupled in Cervantes' proposal for a sequel. It became Sansón's proposal, and eventually decided not only the destination, but indirectly, as we shall see, the duration as well of the third sally.

> ... llegaron a sus oídos relinchos de Rocinante; los cuales relinchos tomó don Quijote por felicísimo agüero, y determinó de hacer de allí a tres o cuatro días otra salida; y declarando su intento al bachiller, le pidió consejo por qué parte comenzaría su jornada;

el cual le respondió que era su parecer que fuese al reino de
Aragón y a la ciudad de Zaragoza, adonde de allí a pocos días se
habían de hacer unas solenísimas justas por la fiesta de San Jorge,
en las cuales podría ganar fama sobre todos los caballeros arago-
neses, que sería ganarla sobre todos los del mundo. II. 4

... the neighing of Rocinante came to his ears, which Don Quijote
took to be most auspicious, and resolved within three or four days
after to make another sally, and, manifesting his mind to the
bachelor, asked his advice to know which way he should begin
his journey; whose opinion was that he should go to the kingdom
of Aragon, and to the city of Zaragoza, where very shortly (within
a few days) there were solemn jousts to be held in the honour
of Saint George, wherein he might get more fame than all the
knights of Aragon, which were above all other knights. II. 4

I take the phrase "*de allí a pocos días*" in the precise
sense. Solemn jousts in honor of Saint George are forthcoming
in Zaragoza. These could only be the festivities in honor of
the Saint's feastday in late April or early May. [16] Hence Cervantes set the scene in the bedchamber and the start of the
third sally in early or mid April. The objective for the third
sally, an event at Zaragoza, is thus convenable to an ensuing
mythical delineation of the hidalgo because provident as a
forthcoming event in the spring of a new year. In other
words, Cervantes' new terms have gathered up the old
and brought them forward on another level. The hidalgo
underwent a rejuvenation of his middle-aged powers at the
start of his first sally. Now, in the third sally, both parody
and exemplary plan are reinforced because rejuvenation is
implied in the season of events and adventures about to
unfold. The hidalgo does not need to imagine or fancy his
outing in the ideal terms of time and place; rather, the
wished-for season with its festivities and landscape is now
provided as a real time and setting. It seems to me all-but-
irrefutable that Cervantes had in mind a date in April for
"solemn jousts in Zaragoza," at least initially. And I even
would go further: initially the entire course of the third sally
was conceived for spring; the festivities in Zaragoza were to
climax and close it. By initially I mean from the time he

completed the First Part in 1604 to the time when the sequel
was well under way in writing.

The demands of exemplary verisimilitude explain why the
action and episodes of the sequel must be immediately
successive to the action of the First Part, yet for the same
reason that action and those episodes must be gathered up
and brought forward onto the new time and setting — spring
of a new year — but as the substance of Don Quijote's fame,
his literary renown in the historical world. This is most
evident from the consequences of Sancho's deception about
his embassy to Dulcinea (I. 30-31). Sancho was persuaded
to invent the story that Dulcinea had requested that Don
Quijote go to see her at El Toboso. Then, in Sierra Morena,
Don Quijote postponed the visit to El Toboso because he
had given his word to the Princess Micomicona to aid her.
Now, in the sequel, that episode stands in the immediate
past, and is the reason why the third sally must open with
the visit to El Toboso. When the pair arrive at the ducal
palace (II. 30-32), the episode of the published First Part
together with events real or imagined in the cave of Montesinos are the basis for the deceptions that follow about
Dulcinea's enchantment and Sancho's lashings. As a fiction,
this line of sequence and consequence must fall within the
limits of duration described by Don Quijote: "Why, my being
about Sierra Morena, and our whole travels were in less than
two months ..." (II. 28).

THE HISTORICAL TIME OF ALONSO QUIJANO

Having traced the connective threads and having set the
scene and time of a third sally for Don Quijote, we may take
up a third perplexity. How specifically did Cervantes draw
the figure of the hidalgo and the accompanying cast of characters against historical events and social conditions in Spain
in his time? Or, does our exemplary plot and its duration
depend to any extent on knowledge or interpretation of
historical events? Here we can discern a single line of practice
that clarifies much of Cervantes' basic design.

The figure of the hidalgo is drawn against a contemporary or historical background consistently, the details infinitesimal, varied, and massive; but that background depicted moves forward as the time and scene of the action from about the year 1589 to 1614. That is to say, though our plot runs its course in the span of months, the duration of the historical scene is twenty-five years. Two premises may be drawn from this. One, the hidalgo Alonso Quijano is contemporary to the time and even the date of the actual composition of the episodes aligned in the narrative of Don Quijote. Two, no specific year can be prescribed for the action, because, though Alonso Quijano is conceived to be about fifty years in age throughout the exemplary plot, the duration (let us say the *temporal distance*) of the historical background is twenty-five years. In the story the hidalgo does indeed age or grow older, but by about a year, certainly not by twenty or twenty-five.

On the one hand Cervantes imagined the life of the hidalgo as an autonomous, poetic or fictional existence, dislodged from the passage of historical time that would age any living person. On the other hand he conceived him as always present or contemporaneous to the particular moment and even the act of composing his story, across the historical interval of twenty years or more. These features cannot be thought of as structural ones in the narrative, yet as a movement of external time sustaining the fictional duration of its plot they may be said to account for the synchronity of our two lines of sequence through a narrative of two summers. In yet another way, however, they do give rise to a structural feature. The recentness of the adventures undergone in the First Part is rendered an immediacy in the Second Part by reason of their having reached published form and a reading audience in the unheard-of interval of one month. The one month of internal, fictional duration corresponds to five or six years of the historical calendar. As a consequence, the two principal lines of plot in the Second Part, Don Quijote's expectations to see Dulcinea in her pristine beauty and Sancho's ambition to rule an island, evolve from the complexities of plot and psychology in the First. To tolerate an interval longer than a year, or even longer than a month, to say nothing of ten years, is to misconstrue the exigencies of exemplary narrative construed by Cervantes for himself.

Yet the exemplary effect is clearly dependent on the truth and insight Cervantes brought to bear on the historical time of his characters. Their story in Part One takes place perforce before 1604; the events spoken of and the everyday life depicted, up to a certain point, pertain to Spain under Philip II. And the action of the sequel takes place after 1609 and the picture is Spain under Philip III. The expulsion of the Moriscos, the picture of Roque Guinart, and the appearance of Avellaneda's spurious copy, are irrefutable evidence that Don Quijote's third sally took place in Cervantes' imagination some ten to twenty years after the first. Is it worthwhile — nay, is it conceivable — to postulate a chronology that will fit the episodes of both Parts into a single sequence and duration, according to both historical evidence and exemplary design? A chronology, that is, resolving the exemplary design of a summer's narrative and its sequel with the historical span of twenty-five years?

This question loomed polemical among Cervantes' critics as the nineteenth century came into being. The dispute centered not on chronology exactly, but on the supposed oversights and negligence of Cervantes, his errors and lapses as exposed by Ríos. The issue may be traced in the commentaries of Juan Antonio Pellicer, Antonio Eximeno, and Diego Clemencín, who, faithful to neoclassical precepts, sought to explain the beauties and wonders of a modern masterpiece in terms of classical models; but the solution was not forthcoming until 1863, from Cervantes' proto-romantic critic.

Pellicer, in 1797, was the first to justify Cervantes' devices for bringing forward, from 1604-05, the time of his sequel to the years of its composition. [17] And like Mayáns he assumed that a date given out in text recorded the day of composition of a given passage: [18] August 22 (I. 25), July 20, 1614 (II. 36), and August 16 (II. 47). Just as Vergil committed a wholesale anachronism in depicting Dido and Aeneas as contemporaries, so Cervantes inverted the times and sequences of his narrative to fit a poetic purpose and design. [19] "The laws of verisimilitude" did not preclude poetic license in the matter of chronology. In the case of an historian anachronisms were unforgivable, but a poet was free to render them fanciful. Moreover, as the authors of chivalric romances perpetrated the worst flaws in chronology, keeping no coherence or cohesion in the order of adventures, so Cervantes, the better to ridicule them in this, even parodied their inconsistencies and loose threads.

The few pages Pellicer devoted to "chronology" and "Duration of the Fable" contrast with the many the querulous Eximeno, a Jesuit priest, musicologist and mathematician, compiled to disprove Ríos. Cervantes reduces historical time, chronology, and duration to a poetical arrangement having a positive antecedent or parallel in the Latin epic and a negative one in the chivalric romances. Certain days and seasons of the year were most appropriate, as time and setting, for elevating a satire of episodic adventure to the scale of the epic. Eximeno followed this basic conception in his polemical *Apología,* published in 1806, [20] but went on to premise for it the novelty of an "imaginary time" derived from Locke's theory of duration. [21]

If real (or true) time, according to Locke (and Eximeno is deriving from the philosopher a distinction between a "real," physical or solar time, and an "imaginary" time of a fable), consists in the succession of ideas passing through our minds while we are awake, the "imaginary time" of the fable consists of the succession of ideas that this fable presents to our understanding. [22] It is this "imaginary succession of ideas," or "objects" or events that comprise its action. In *Don Quijote* the time and duration of the action is of "the same nature as the fable ... imaginary," [23] and exempt from calculations by the calendar or the almanac. Within that imaginary succession, unaffected by the passage of years, the season was fixed as a summer or arcadian spring. Hence the action, a series of loosely related episodes, could not be confined to any historical date, for the train of events from beginning to end was independent of historical sequence and dates, even those put in the text. [24] Cervantes had even foreseen "the chronologies and calculations" that his fable would thereafter attract, and reserved his scorn for Ríos and the like.

Cervantes had not had a more truculent apologist than this Jesuit; he ranged triumphantly where Ríos failed abjectly, over the span and season of the sequel, with its unlikely connective of one month. Here Eximeno came upon a major "structural" discovery about the festivals mentioned. They are all spring festivals, [25] but ordered in such a way that the only consistency they point to is a fanciful spring season to match the festive styles of a mock history of chivalry. Don Quijote's arrival at Barcelona on Saint John's Day was obviously one of those "ideas in train." [26] Ríos' only notion had been an exact chronology by the calendar, and dated it 30 November. How could Cervantes' description of the dawn on this day be dated in November, by any rule of verisimilitude? Eximeno was clearly within sight of Don Quijote's mythical orb, yet by what means did he come upon these insights?

Strangely, but like so many apologists and polemicists, he owes his brightest intuitions to the prodding of an obsession to demolish his rival. Implacably he pored over, one by one, those errors or inconsistencies in the itinerary of Don Quijote's adventures, geography, and chronology uncovered by Ríos, and turned up, almost in the spirit of spite, a precious few insights. He fathomed the artistic relation between Don Quijote's illusion of himself as knight and the temporal motion depicted by the styles of his fable. But, intent on reducing Ríos' Plan to nonsense, he never came to grips with the unity of the work he defended almost fanatically. Don Quijote himself does not emerge from his pages as a meaningful character. If the unified lines of the fable in *Don Quijote* were those of an epic in prose, their purpose never clarified into

the significance of an original form, in plot, characters, or
style. In other words, he did not think of it as a novel. Looking
across the sweep of Cervantes' parodies, he felt the impulse
to follow their curve of suggestion between the dates of the
spring festivals in the third sally and to premise therefrom a
perpetual, arcadian spring as a setting, but the prospect, the
expedient, was for him familiar, — satire and the mock heroic,
a rational concession of the poet Cervantes to the substance
of the thing parodied. The full sweep of Cervantes' parodies
along that curve would have drawn for him an hidalgo's
mythical spring.

DIARIO: 1863

Nothing else about it reveals so overtly the enterprise
Juan Eugenio Hartzenbusch undertook for *Don Quijote* as
the "Diary" fashioned "for the better intelligence of his expeditions and adventures," and only a publisher's inspiration
to print and publish the book in the very room where Cervantes had conceived it (supposedly while imprisoned in
Argamasilla de Alba) could hope to match it. [27] But equally
by it the proclivity and artistic tastes of an era are defined
and also betrayed. For Hartzenbusch was a man to bring to
an editor's tasks the sensibility of a genuine poet, and
to redefine for his contemporaries the poetic wealth stored in
the masterpiece. [28] He presumed to entertain a lofty conception of both history and poetry, and offered in the "Diary" a
distillation of both. He was overwhelmingly attracted by what
we have called the diurnal and natural rhythm of Cervantes'
story, and conceived that these beauties offered to the
beholder a grand unfolding of poetic detail clarified into
the picturesque transparency of everyday life.

It takes an effort on our part to understand, let alone
recapture, the feeling for the everyday historical that stirred
him and other nineteenth-century readers. For them it seemed
a marvel that in *Don Quijote* one might imagine the year
1589 as so many hours of daylight, nights, months and seasons,
having the full force of reality as, say, the year 1859. And so

it seemed a delight, and a discovery, to him to be able to
fix the historical dates of Don Quijote's sallies down to the
day of the week. Yet, lest one be misled, that historical image
of time was eminently poetical, because it restored to Cervantes' pages the fancy of ingenious inspiration. In other
words, the "Diary" was poetry extracted by a solicitous
criticism.

Hartzenbusch contemplated the chronological record in
Don Quijote from both above and afar; he recognized that
the spans of two summers and the historical span of twenty-
five years from 1589 to 1614 must be accounted for, and, fixing
the diurnal order of the episodes according to some immutable
dates, sought to reconcile the greatest number of inconsistencies and oversights in chronology by justification of the
most palpable one. Unintimidated by the failure or success
of his predecessors, Ríos, Pellicer, Eximeno, and Clemencín,
he was emboldened to outstrip their theses at precisely the
most sensitive points.

Of the various possible dates for the action of the first
summer he chose the year 1589, no doubt because the historical reference to the Duke of Alba in the captain's story
(I. 39) dispelled all doubts. The dates of the two years 1589
and 1614 were for him incontrovertible evidence and must
be accepted as such, but the interval between them need not
count positively as twenty-five years; it was a span of time
used mockingly, poetic license, in a mock history of chivalry.
Here in part is his preface to the "Diary."

> Taking as a basis the historical events mentioned in the course
> of the narrative, the action of Part One corresponds to the year
> 1589; the action of the second takes place in the year 1614. Those
> twenty five years that in fact intervened between them are thus
> reduced in the novel to one, two, or three at the most, whether
> because the author considered history as a fable when he used it
> in a work of pure invention, or whether because he desired to
> expose with one colossal anachronism the many to be found in
> romances of chivalry and the plays of the period...
>
> The year 1589 began and ended on a Sunday; the year 1614
> began on a Wednesday: in order to splice them, and make Wednes-
> day fall immediately after Sunday, one must use the same poetic

license Cervantes employed for narrowing the gap between them or suppose that three years had gone by since Don Quijote returned to his village, before he ventured forth on a third and last sally.

Within the year 1589, the diary of Part One is based on three dates; first, Don Quijote made his first sally on a Friday in July, when, at nightfall, there was moonlight. These circumstances correspond perfectly to Friday, July 28, 1589. The second is the date of the warrant made out by Don Quijote, and the third is based on the fact that he returned to his village on a Sunday, six days after rogations for rain. The warrant is dated August 22 in the first and second editions of Cuesta, and in the third, August 27, a discrepancy that indicates difficulty and doubt, and perhaps error, in reading numbers in Cervantes' original. Hence, so that Don Quijote's entry into Argamasilla may fall on the second Sunday of September 1589, the letter has been dated August 30.

Part Two offers three important dates, duly respected here; the rest, for the contradictions they would introduce, have been disregarded. Don Quijote sallies forth from Argamasilla with Sancho two days before the octave of Corpus Christi, a festival falling that year (1614) on May 29, and the octave, consequently on June 5; Sancho writes a letter to his wife on July 20; Don Quijote enters Barcelona on Saint John's Day, that is, the day of his Martyrdom, August 29.

Taking these three fixed dates, Hartzenbusch arranged the episodes in the sequel in a succession running from June to the end of September, overlooking any number of contradictory points. His Diary is an improvement over Ríos' Plan only in that it provides a summer period for the time of the sequel. As a reconstruction of order, duration, and coherence, by nineteenth-century tastes in historical realism and verisimilitude in fiction, it is not unmeaningful. As literary criticism it is a misconception. Having failed to understand Cervantes' connective of "one month" it followed that he would fail to see two strands of temporal duration — an exemplary and a mythical strand — drawing together the historical span of twenty-five years of external time and duration, and nullifying the entire idea of a uniformity of succession. What Hartzenbusch plotted is a uniform chronological sequence that will place Don Quijote's arrival at Barcelona at the end of summer, as shown on the second gyre of our configuration.

Both the Plan and the Diary were assembled and justified as repairs on oversights of a careless or harried author. The idea may have struck our two chronologers that Cervantes had shaped his narrative toward a goal acquiescent but not subservient to chronological order, but to admit as much, or as little, would have left the improvidence of their time-schemes exposed. Neither could cope with arrival at Barcelona at midsummer. Their search for outward uniformity would only conceal from them an interior movement dependent on the progressive enlargement of Don Quijote's mythical fame. But it could have made no sense to them that Don Quijote's adventures are timed for a spring-like summer, or what amounts to the same thing, that the time of arrival at Barcelona might revert to midsummer. One feels that, even had Hartzenbusch found a clue in romances of chivalry, he might not have recognized it (he even passed over the evidence in Clemencín's notes [29]), so sure was he about Cervantes' intentions. "¡San Juan después de Julio! ¡después del 16 de Agosto! ¡Qué anacronismo!" [30] Of course no anachronism was there; Cervantes had had in mind the festival of Saint John's Martyrdom, on Friday, August 29, 1614. At least two contemporary commentator-critics, Arturo Marasso and Martín de Riquer, would agree with him that Cervantes had the festival of Saint John's Martyrdom in mind. [31]

Hartzenbusch believed that by rendering the historical in Don Quijote authentic by the almanac he was fulfilling Cervantes' precept for resolving a mock history of chivalry — historia burlesca de caballerías — on the level of an authentic historical record. The "colossal anachronism," if not deliberate, was at least half-conscious artistry. Like Ríos he could not accept the techniques of parody of a chronicle of chivalric feats as serious literary enterprise. The scattered, inchoate details must be assembled and reconstructed on the side of genuine history, that is, the perspective several centuries later back upon a scene contemplated as an historical present.

THE CHRONOLOGY OF MOCK CHIVALRY

On the orb of myth of our configuration the span of temporal duration of the sequel runs from the vernal equinox to midsummer. An exemplary strand places the start of the third sally in early April and follows a course traceable through June and beyond, into July-August, according to Cervantes' dates. Yet it is moving parallel to the other, a strand whose course runs from spring to midsummer and traces the arc of a mythical time for Don Quijote's history. Thus his arrival at Barcelona appears verisimilar at the end of August by a chronological progression, but incumbent at midsummer by the time and season of his mythical history.

According to our exemplary strand, arrival at Barcelona in Chapter 61 could coincide with Hartzenbusch's chronological scheme, for he traced what we have called the second line of narrative movement in the sequel, yet he misconceived it as exclusively chronological. He had the evidence before him pointing to the liaison between the initial chapters of the Second Part, up to Chapter 29, and the closing chapters, after Chapter 59, where the season is spring moving toward summer, and to the interval separating them, Don Quijote's long stay in the ducal palace. Our exemplary strand moves the initial adventures of the sequel through spring and a spring-like summer; thereon, events in the ducal palace, Chapters 30-58, take place in July and August, but when Don Quijote and Sancho leave the palace and make their way to Barcelona, the season reverts to spring, and the two strands are aligned at midsummer. The adventures of the second summer thus fall into three phases, and the liaison between the first and the third is a key to this alignment. That liaison is apparent in various ways. Two may be mentioned here. The interval of time between the octave of Corpus Christi (II. 11) and Saint John's Nativity (II. 61) suggests the initial scheme for the sequel. The other is the alignment of dawn descriptions, with their burlesque parodies, pointed along the arc of a mythical spring for Don

Quijote's outings. Each of these sunrises evokes the arcadian spring of the golden age.

> Scarce had the silver morn given bright Phoebus leave, with the ardour of his burning rays, to dry the liquid pearls on his golden locks, when Don Quijote, shaking off sloth from his drowsy members, rose up, and called Sancho his squire, that still lay snorting . . .
> II. 20

A chronicle of mock chivalry, however it defers to dates and historical events by the calendar, must follow the lofty desiderate of a solar delineation for the hero's course; for by that course a mythical spring and a mythical summer are both fulfilled, as it were, at midsummer. Cervantes had perforce to locate his exemplary narrative in a given place and time, and to specify the pathological condition of his hero by them. But the psychosis of his hero is an abnormity of literary proportions. Of course the mythical career of the mock hero is centered in the psychosis of Alonso Quijano. Of course the mythical history adumbrated in the mock chivalry is delusion, a mirage of literary styles. Why, then, we ask, as an imperative of his parody, did Cervantes depict Don Quijote's arrival at Barcelona at midsummer, after a course of adventures that take place in July and August?

That is, why must Saint John's Day, June 24, serve to bring to a climax the course of chivalric adventures through a summer immediately preceding, as if this feast day climaxed the course of spring from April and May to midsummer? The answer is to be found in a most decisive, and subtle, difference between the First and Second Parts. We can say, for the sake of brevity, that Don Quijote's fame in Part One is limited by the framework of exemplary narrative, its orbit confined to the psychotic imagination of a deranged hero. And this is the way it strikes those closest to him and inclined to humor him, the priest, the barber, Dorotea. But in the sequel the fame of Don Quijote is a fact of the real world, of Cervantes' world, with the momentous consequence that as the *ingenioso hidalgo* goes forth for a third round of adventures his fame as *ingenioso caballero* precedes him, creating an unprecedented spectacle whereby a literary character invested with a living renown becomes the "living" character with a mythical fame. Sansón Carrasco, on seeing him in the flesh for the first time, recognizes the knight famed in and out of his *history*.

> ... en viendo a don Quijote, poniéndose delante dél de rodillas, diciéndole: —Deme vuestra grandeza las manos, señor don Quijote de la Mancha ... que es vuestra merced uno de los más famosos caballeros andantes que ha habido, ni aun habrá, en toda la redondez de la tierra. II. 3

Sansón is the first of a line of celebrators of his prowess; on arrival at Barcelona, the equally burlesque and bantering don Antonio Moreno comes forward to greet a fabled knight:

> —Bien sea venido a nuestra ciudad el espejo, el farol, la estrella y el norte de toda la caballería andante, donde más largamente se contiene. Bien sea venido, digo, el valeroso don Quijote de la Mancha ... II. 61
>
> —*Welcome to our city is the looking-glass, the lanthorn, and north star of all knight-errantry, where it is most in practice! Welcome, I say, is the valorous Don Quijote de la Mancha ...!* II. 61

The "mythical time" of Don Quijote is the advent of felicitous fame. The seasonal course of the third sally adumbrates that felicitous future time announced mockingly at the outset of the first sally. Preceded by the fame gained at the expense of his exploits in Part One, for he is known by them to multitudes, Don Quijote goes forth in expectation of fulfilling those psychotic longings in a time and season of his mythical renown. Accordingly, the stage and scale for that delineation are magnificent, in contrast to the paltry inns and fields of the episodes of Part One. And Cervantes, equal to the challenge, will devise a scale for his mock-heroic romance to fit a depiction of contemporary society along epical lines. Don Quijote's festive entry into Barcelona, and

the mock ovation lavished on him, will be the crowning event
of an adventurous course reaching back from El Toboso and
the cave of Montesinos to the ducal palace, flight on Clavileño, and the winning of Barataria by Sancho. Thus the time
and duration of the sequel are pointed, beyond their chronology of days and dates, or a span of historical years and
events, towards the hour of felicitous fame, the morning of
Saint John's Day. As a literary time and duration that hour
is the happy future time of his first expectation: ". . . offering
himself to occasions and dangers . . . once happily achieved,
might gain him eternal renown" (I. 1).

Mythical fame, impugned as illusion, feeds on expectation
and successive recognition; its advent is what temporal
duration enacts and fulfills. By virtue of it an exemplary and
historical time becomes mythical time. Reaching back into
the first summer, it gathers adventures just recently accomplished and projects them into the second summer. Because
that fame, configured outward from psychosis to exploits, is
mythical, its temporal duration is magical and prophetic.
Thus, if the narrative of Part Two brings forward the adventures of Part One, and makes the first summer immediately
previous, the action and exemplary sequence of Part One
remain the narrative focus in the sequel and the second
summer becomes, as well as consecutive, synchronous (as
shown in our configuration) to the first. Without an intervening
winter, the season becomes late spring and summer, exemplary for its duration and end, mythical in its immunity to
the passage of time, to effects of age, and true to wish
fulfillment. Thus in the second summer of the sequel Don
Quijote's trajectory describes a curve suggestive of the solar
cycle; he is linked with the feast days of Saint George in
April, Corpus Christi in May, Saint John's in June (and, for
some, in August); [32] recognized, celebrated, as the famous
Manchegan knight, the season and landscape of his 'history'
are, by parody and allusion, the fanciful spring and summer
of romance.

NOTES TO CHAPTER II

1. Consult M[auricio] de Iriarte, *El doctor Huarte de San Juan y su "Examen de ingenios," contribución a la historia de la psicología diferencial* (Madrid: C. S. I. C., 1948, 3rd ed.), pp. 311-322. Otis H. Green, "El *ingenioso* hidalgo," *Hispanic Review,* 25: 175-193 (1957), and a comprehensive discussion in *Spain and the Western Tradition* (Univ. of Wisconsin Press, 1963-64, 4 vols.), IV, pp. 60-73, 258-261; collected in *The Literary Mind of Medieval and Renaissance Spain* (Univ. Press of Kentucky, 1970), pp. 155-184.

2. See my article "The Summer of Myth," *Philological Quarterly,* 51: 145-157 (1972); p. 146.

3. See discussion on *"verano:* 'tiempo primaveral' " in J. Corominas, *Diccionario crítico etimológico de la lengua castellana* (Madrid: Gredos, 1954), IV, s.v., *verano.* In *DQ* Cervantes seems to have preferred *verano* where *estío* would be in order: "el caballero... resista en los páramos despoblados los ardientes rayos del sol en la mitad del *verano,* y en el *invierno* la dura inclemencia de los vientos y de los yelos" II. 17; cf. the passage from II. 53, quoted p. 158. From Covarrubias (1611) a description of a division into four seasons (where "Primavera" would be the fifth: *"Primavera...* la entrada del verano, 882. b. 32): "entrando el sol en Aries [March 21], empieza el verano; en Cancro [June 22], el estío; en Libra [Sept. 23], el autumo; en Capricornio [Dec. 22], la hieme, o el invierno," 566. a. 21. Sebastián de Covarrubias, *Tesoro de la lengua castellana o española,* ed. Riquer (Barcelona, 1943). For *Persiles y Sigismunda* see J. B. Avalle-Arce, ed. Castalia (Madrid, 1969), note, p. 222.

In English the simplest meaning of *summer* is, of course, "the warmest half of the year," and implies a division of only two seasons. The popular use of the term, as in the folklore of the peoples of the northern hemisphere, has conceived *summer* to be the period from May 1st or mid-May to mid-August (see *Oxford English Dictionary),* which would account for 'Midsummer Day' on June 21st or 24th.

4. The *omission* of an account of certain adventures deemed not worthy or important was part of a stylistic temporal formula in the Spanish *libros de caballerías,* with antecedents in Arthurian romance. Cervantes' originality and satire lie in the fact his character is highly aware of the total blank this day is in an account of his chivalry. Cf. these examples: "Partido Palmerín de la corte del emperador su agüelo en compañía de la doncella de Tracia, algunas aventuras halló de que *aquí no se hace mención por ser de poca calidad.* Assi que, *dejando de contar* algunas cosas que en aquella jornada passó, dice la historia que... ," *Palmerín de Inglaterra,* ed. Bonilla y San Martín (Madrid, 1908), NBAE, vol. 11, p. 177. "Pues así anduuo [Beltenebrós] fasta la noche, que aluergó en casa de vn cauallero anciano... y otro día, partiendo dende ... anduuo siete días *sin ninguna auentura fallar;* mas a los ocho ...", *Amadís de Gaula,* ed. Edwin B. Place (Madrid: C. S. I. C., 1959-1971, 4 vols.), Bk. II, Ch. 55, p. 452a. "Y otro día caminaron *sin cosa que de contar sea les acaeçiesse* hasta que

llegaron a Uindilisora, donde era el rey Lisuarte," *Amadís de Gaula,* Bk, I, Ch. 13, p. 114a. "Fueron quinze días *sin que aventura les viniesse que de contar sea,*" *Amadís de Grecia,* Bk. 2, Ch. 22. This and other examples cited by John Bowle, *DQ* [I. 2], *Anotaciones,* p. 14.

In *Amadís de Gaula,* as in all medieval works, the passage of time is marked by the canonical hours, with the characteristic phrases of Arthurian romance. See W. Rothwell, "The Hours of the Day in Medieval French," *French Studies,* 13: 240-251 (1959).

5. See entries for *tiempo, hora* in Carlos Fernández Gómez, *Vocabulario de Cervantes* (Madrid: Real Academia Española, 1962). *Reloj* (clock), as a time piece, is mentioned variously in *Persiles y Sigismunda,* but in *Don Quijote* only once, "concertado reloj" (first paragraph of I. 33), a metaphor recalling the famous one by Antonio de Guevara "la vida del príncipe no es sino un reloj que concierta toda la república," *Reloj de príncipes,* Prólogo general (1529).

6. See Otis H. Green, *Spain and the Western Tradition,* IV, pp. 22-42.

7. Mayáns, "The Life of . . . Cervantes," in vol. 1 of Charles Jarvis' translation of *Don Quijote* (London: J. and R. Tonson, 1742), #101, p. 52. The original, in Spanish, was published in 1737.

8. "In one thing Cervantes ought to be treated with some Rigour, and that is in the Anachronisms or Retrocessions of time; for having himself so greatly reflected upon his Contemporary Play-wrights in this particular, such Defects ought to be censured in him" (#102). Mayáns then proceeded to enumerate all "anachronisms" and found so many he gave up in futility (#126). Clearly it was impossible to compute a duration for such a story. A more reasonable approach was taken by John Bowle some forty years later. Bowle (in his *Anotaciones*) simply noted antecedents and similarities he found in books Cervantes ridiculed and let them speak for themselves. He deduced that the duration of the action throughout Parts One and Two was *ten* years, from the two statements about the housekeeper's age in I. 1 ("over forty") and II. 73 ("fifty years"), *Anotaciones,* Part Two, p. 164. On Bowle as commentator see Ralph Merrit Cox, *The Rev. John Bowle, The Genesis of Cervantean Criticism,* University of North Carolina Studies in Romance Languages and Literatures, Num. 99 (Chapel Hill, 1971), Chs. 4 and 5.

9. "Plan cronológico del *Quijote,*" in "Juicio crítico o análisis del *Quijote,*" vol. I of ed. publ. by Real Academia Española, Madrid, 1780. See also #18-20, 288, 323, 324 of the *Análisis.*

10. See notes (Comentario) to his ed., espec. I, pp. 23, 38 [I. 2], notes 5 and 45. In subsequent reprints of the Comentario the notes to each of the chapters are numbered.

11. The English version quoted in my extracts was published as part of prefatory matter (author/translator anonymous) in an ed. of Jarvis' translation, vol. I (London: William Miller, 1804, 4 vols.).

12. ". . . se puede inferir que Cervantes no consultó su primera parte al tiempo de escribir su segunda, contentándose con suponer

que sucedió esta en la estación más oportuna para los acaecimientos que en ella se refieren, esto es, en el verano" (#327).

13. *Reisebilder IV, Italien, Die Stadt Lucca* (1830), *Sämtl. Wk.*, hg. O. Walzel (Leipzig, 1910-1915), vol. 5, pp. 63-66. I have quoted a translation of the passage by S. L. Fleishman, *Prose Writings of Heinrich Heine*, ed. Havelock Ellis (London: Walter Scott, 1887), pp. 243-245. Heine reproduced the passage in his "Einleitung zum *Don Quijote*," the prefatory to a translation published in Stuttgart in 1837. The passage is the source for the misconception about who in disguise defeated Don Quijote. Heine remembered it was Sansón Carrasco, but didn't remember that Sansón was a *bachiller*, not a barber-surgeon. Dostoievsky repeated the error in another famous passage. "Who was it — Heine, was it not? — who recounted how, as a boy, he had burst into tears when, reading Don Quixote he had reached the place where the hero was conquered by the despicable and common-sense barber-surgeon Samson Carrasco," *The Diary of a Writer*, trans. Boris Brasol (London, 1949), I, p. 260.

14. On the connective of "almost one month," cf. Joaquín Casalduero, *Sentido y forma del "Quijote"* (Madrid. Insula, 1970, p. 215.

15. The very general kind of information available would allow one to infer that Cervantes began to write the Second Part, at the very earliest, in 1607; but the year 1609 seems just as likely. See note 37 to Ch. 3 below.

16. Commenting on this point in Eximeno's arguments (see p. 58 and note 20 below) Clemencín [II. 4] IV, p. 77, note 13 and also [II. 59] VI, p. 211, note 58, cited the notice by Jerónimo de Urrea (from Pellicer, Parte Primera, Tomo III), the translator to Spanish of the *Orlando furioso*, that jousts in honor of Saint George were held on three different occasions throughout the year in Zaragoza. "Sabed que los caballeros desta ciudad tienen una Cofradía en memoria de su Patrón San Jorge, y es que son obligados a justar tres veces en el año, y a tornear a caballo otras tantas...," *Diálogo de la verdadera honra militar* (1556), folio 76, quoted by Ricardo del Arco y Garay, *La sociedad española en las obras de Cervantes* (Madrid, 1951), p. 357. See also the notes Juan Givanel Mas brought together in vol. 6 of Cortejón's ed. *Don Quijote*, p. 196. I think it is quite clear from the text that Cervantes had in mind only one occasion for Don Quijote to show up in Zaragoza and not the possibility of several, e.g., "They mounted their beasts and followed the road to Zaragoza, where they expected to arrive in time to be present at a solemn festival which is held every year in that illustrious city," II. 10. Saint George's Day (April 23) in the Middle Ages was celebrated throughout Europe as a spring festival, in religious observances and folk rituals and pastimes. See *Enciclopedia Cattolica* VI (1951), pp. 443-444.

17. See Section IV of "Discurso Preliminar" to his ed., Parte Primera, Tomo I and description of Don Quijote's itinerary, Parte Segunda, Tomo II, pp. 437-468.

18. Parte Segunda, Tomo II, p. 82, note; and Clemencín, Comentario [II. 36] V, p. 248, note 21, [II. 47] V, p. 442, note 35.

19. "Cervantes pues para ridiculizar con mayor propiedad los libros de caballerías, quiso parece conformarse con su estilo en todo, alterando, invirtiendo, estrechando o dilatando el espacio y la serie de los tiempos, reduciéndolos a una masa cronológica por decirlo así, de donde entresacó el conveniente para la duración de la fábula, y para que tuviesen cabimiento todas las proezas y sucesos de su héroe, eligiendo aquellos días y estaciones más apacibles y oportunas para la ejecución de sus aventuras," "Discurso Preliminar," Parte Primera, Tomo I, p. xxxi.

20. Eximeno [y Pujades], Antonio, *Apología de Miguel de Cervantes sobre los yerros que se le han notado en el "Quixote."* (Madrid: Imp. de la Administración del Real Arbitrio, 1806).

21. Locke's remarks on duration appear in Ch. 14 of *An Essay concerning Human Understanding* (1690). They have been accounted for as a source for Sterne's time-scheme in *Tristram Shandy,* see note 3 to Ch. 1 above (Baird).

22. "Diximos ya que el tiempo de la acción de una fábula es de la misma naturaleza de ella, esto es, fabuloso e imaginario; y la cronología del tiempo imaginario no debe calcularse por los calendarios y diarios de tiempo verdadero. El tiempo verdadero, dice el filósofo Lock, y dice bien, consiste en la verdadera sucesión de ideas, que, durante la vigilia, pasan por nuestra mente, y aun por eso en la eternidad no hay tiempo, porque no hay sucesión de ideas (p. 60)." "El tiempo imaginario de una fábula consiste en la sucesión de ideas que presenta la misma fábula, y es un error el quererle determinar y medir con la medida del tiempo verdadero; sino medirse debe por la sucesión de los objetos, de que se compone la acción de la fábula (p. 61)."

23. Eximeno, pp. 19-20, 24, 111.

24. Eximeno, p. 75.

25. Eximeno, pp. 132-133.

26. Eximeno, pp. 67-68, 122-124.

27. Juan Eugenio Hartzenbusch (1806-1880) published his edition of *Don Quijote* separately and, also, as part of Cervantes' *Obras completas* in 1863, both in Argamasilla de Alba. The publisher set up his presses in the room where Cervantes was supposedly confined. The "Diario" follows the editor's Prologue in vol. I. The translation of the preface is mine.

28. Hartzenbusch is, of course, best known as a dramatist of the Romantic period in Spain. He wrote several plays based on historical legends, among them *Los amantes de Teruel* (1837) and *La jura en Santa Gadea* (1845).

29. Clemencín, Comentario [II. 62] VI, p. 259 note 2.

30. Hartzenbusch, Note to II. 61, vol. 4, p. 346.

31. Arturo Marasso, *Cervantes, la invención del "Quijote"* (Buenos Aires: Libr. Hachette, 1954), p. 36. Martín de Riquer, ed., *Don Quijote* (Barcelona: Editorial Planeta, 1967) [II. 60], note, p. 1049.

32. See Marasso, op. cit., "Don Quijote en el ciclo solar de las fiestas del año," pp. 35-36; "Don Quijote precedido por la fama," pp. 107-108. Marasso linked Don Quijote's arrival at Barcelona with the festival of Isis (a spring festival) and assumed Cervantes had committed a more or less intentional anachronism.

III

THE CHRONOLOGY OF COMPOSITION

"ÉSTE HARÁ VEINTE Y DOS AÑOS QUE SALÍ DE CASA DE MI PADRE"

> There lived not long since, in a certain village of the Mancha
> (the name whereof I do not now recall), a gentleman of their calling
> that used to pile up in their halls old lances, halberds, morions, and
> such other armours and weapons. He was, besides, master of an
> ancient target, a lean stallion, and a swift greyhound. His pot
> consisted daily of somewhat more beef than mutton ... I. 1

The enduring phrases are similar to the opening passage
in two other narratives by Cervantes. [1] One of them is the
narrative of the captive captain, Ruy Pérez, in Chapter 39
of Part One:

> In a certain village of the mountains of Leon my lineage had
> beginning, wherewithal nature dealt much more liberally than for-
> tune, although my father had the opinion, amidst the penury and
> poverty of that people, to be a rich man, as indeed he might have
> been, had he but used as much care to hoard up his wealth as
> prodigality to spend it. I. 39

El ingenioso hidalgo, El celoso extremeño; these passages,
their title (and also *El curioso impertinente*), and other
similarities in the three narratives define a phase in Cervantes'
development as a writer. Almost certainly this phase represents his earliest efforts in what he was to offer to the public
in 1613 as *novelas ejemplares.* The beginning of this phase,
one may conjecture, was about the year 1589 and its close
about the year 1599, when the original conception for *El
ingenioso hidalgo* transcended the design of a short narrative
and took on the full attributes of a mock history of chivalry. [2]

The opening passage in the captain's story, told before a
gathering in the inn, leads up to an account of a separation
of sons from the father, and to this disclosure (romans mine):

This will be the twenty-second year *since I left my father's house, and in all this time and although I have written a number of letters* (algunas cartas), *I have had no word of him or of my brothers. And as to my experiences in the course of this time I shall relate them briefly. I embarked from Alicante, I arrived prosperously at Genoa, and from thence went to Milan, where I did accommodate myself with arms and other braveries used by soldiers, and departed from thence to settle myself in Piedmont; and being in my way towards the city of Alexandria de la Paglia, I heard news that the great Duke of Alba did pass towards Flanders. Wherefore, changing my purpose, I went with him, and served him in all the expeditions he made. I. 39*

The Duke of Alba made the journey to Flanders in 1567, arriving in Brussels on August 22. [3] The present time of the telling of this "historical" tale, the scene in the inn, would then be the year 1589, twenty-two years later. On May 21 in 1590 in Seville Cervantes submitted a petition to the Crown requesting an administrative post in the New World. It begins:

Miguel de çerbantes sahauedra dice que ha seruido a V.M. muchos años en las jornadas de mar y tierra que se han ofrescido *de veinte y dos años* a e_ta parte, particularmente en la Batalla Naual, donde le dieron muchas heridas, de las quales perdio vna mano de vn arcabuçaco — y el año siguiente fue a Nauarino y despues a la de Tunez y a la goleta ... [4]

Miguel de Cervantes Saavedra says he has served Your Majesty many years on expeditions on land and sea in the course of twenty-two years *to this date, particularly in the Naval Battle [i.e., Lepanto], where he received many wounds, and lost [the use of] a hand from an arcabuz shot — and the next year [1572] he went to Navarino and then to Tunis and to la Goleta ...*

There can be little doubt that the opening passage of the captain's story is nearly contemporaneous to this document. According to the latter, Cervantes in 1590 had been in the king's military service since 1568 but it seems he calculated from the time he left Spain for Italy, not the year of his enlistment. [5] He enlisted in Italy, probably in 1570, having made his way there under obscure circumstances the previous year. [6] The captain's story begins as a narrative of military service and historical events taking place from 1567 to 1573; it parallels somewhat the course of Cervantes' fortunes as a soldier and the years of Algerian captivity (1575-1580). As we shall see, the span of "twenty-two" years into the past is not an incidental detail in a romantic story of an escape to freedom and reunion. The author Cervantes was looking back on the eventful decade of his youth in the year 1589 or 1590, after a decade of unfulfilled hopes. This retrospection gives us the date 1589 for the captive's narrative, at least for the initial portions, but its appearance in chapters 39, 40, and 41 belongs to a later phase of narrative development, the final phase of the years 1603-04. Cervantes then intercalated into his episodic plot a story conceived and written some fourteen years earlier.

The dates proposed by Hartzenbusch for the action, 1589 and 1614, span the twenty-five year process, if not of the book's composition, then of the germination and growth of the initial idea and its evolution in the mind of Cervantes. Perhaps no other literary masterpiece so palpably exposes, whether by design or default, the process of its evolution from a provisional to a great idea. That process moved forward in phases, each one unexpectedly and as if by experiment confirming the richness and novelty of the initial conception.

Now, certain inconsistencies or perplexities in plot, theme, or style, and in duration and 'chronology,' can be explained for the variance between the order of composition of some episodes or passages in Part I and their arrangement or interpolation within the overall sequence. The passages quoted above from the captain's narrative belong to a phase of composition antedating even the initial idea for an exemplary narrative about a Manchegan hidalgo, but their interpolation in that narrative belongs to the last phase (up to 1604). The actual writing of the main narrative probably took place in the years 1598-1604 for the First Part and 1609-1614 for the Second. Two and perhaps three of the intercalated narratives in the First were composed separately, and before

Cervantes had thought out a plan for the entire narrative: "The Story of the Captive Captain" and "The Curious Impertinent." Ruy Pérez's disclosure about "twenty-two years" is the only detail providing anything like a specific historical date for the plot of Don Quijote's first summer; but of numerous allusions in Part I that fit the course of the action into the contemporary scene up to the date of publication, it is the earliest. All things considered, the most plausible date for the action of Part I would be a summer in the years 1592 to 1598; the first date is the earliest one could include a book published in 1591, *Iberia's Shepherd,* in the hidalgo's library (I. 6); the second is the last summer king Philip II (died 13 September 1598) could have been spoken of as alive and reigning, as in the scene in the inn in Chapter 39. The latest acquisitions in the hidalgo's library by date of publication are a group of books published after Cervantes' *Galatea,* 1585, and before 1592. [7]

Our inquiry has emphasized that one ingredient in Cervantes' basic design — or his *invention* — is that its episodes are imagined by him as practically contemporaneous to the time, — that is, the scene and historical reality, of their composition. Add this ingredient to the others — an exemplary plan and fable, an episodic plot for a parody of chivalric adventures, scope and variety in interpolated tales and their characters — and one can make out the consequences that a chronological order for the composition of his episodes or their interpolation may have had on the overall design of a summer period as the literary duration for that complexity and wealth. We shall speak of phases of development and composition, and hopefully seek to illuminate the narrative of two consecutive summers by hypothesizing, on the basis of the known facts, the chronological outline of those phases.

THE FIVE PHASES OF PART ONE
"BIEN COMO QUIEN SE ENGENDRÓ EN UNA CÁRCEL ..."

Y así, ¿qué podrá engendrar el estéril y mal cultivado ingenio mío sino la historia de un hijo seco, avellanado, antojadizo y lleno

de pensamientos varios y nunca imaginados de otro alguno, bien
como quien se engendró en una cárcel, donde toda incomodidad
tiene su asiento y donde todo triste ruido hace su habitación? (Prólogo, 1604).

*And thus, what could my sterile and ill-tilled wit engender but
the history of a dry-toasted and humorous son, full of various
thoughts and conceits never before imagined of any other; much
like one who was engendered within some noisome prison, where all
discommodities have taken possession, and all doleful noises made
their habitation?*

We do not need to accept as literal truth the statement
that he conceived the story of Don Quijote in a prison. It
suffices by way of a symbolical declaration. Cervantes suffered
the humiliation of a brief imprisonment in Castro del Río in
1592. He was again confined in the Royal Prison in Seville
for several months in 1597. [8] This long confinement has all
the marks of an appalling turn of fortune, for one inured to
adversity. *El ingenioso hidalgo* is the book Cervantes conceived when it appeared hopeless to pursue a career as a
writer. Whether it was conceived or written within the walls
of the Royal Prison of Seville, or of any other, remains a
supposition, but with an undeniable symbolical import; for
it was surely conceived in an hour of trial, affliction, and
uncertainty, in the deepest recesses of personal consciousness. [9] The book, new to him and to the world in 1604, was
an affirmation of imaginative genius over despair. Yet another
event in the following year seems to me of almost equal
importance: the death of king Philip II. If confinement
produced inner search and self-discovery, the passing of the
only monarch Spain had known throughout nearly all of
Miguel's life brought a release of pent-up feelings and
hesitations. A hitherto reserved side of his artistic nature
found liberation: the ironic attitude towards the political life,
sentiments, and manners of a fading century and its military
glories. The author of the artificial *Galatea* recedes in plain
view of the mocking author of the famous sonnet penned to
commemorate the catafalque for Philip's exequies in Seville. [10]

My guess is that ideas for a story about a Manchegan hidalgo had come to Cervantes in various guises and on occasions between 1590 and 1597, in the course of his travels and exasperating ordeals as commissary in Andalusia; then in 1597 and 1598 he put them into a draft form along the lines of an exemplary narrative. But as he did so the idea flourished unexpectedly, so that after 1599 he projected a much longer form for it, and subsequently divided it into Parts and Chapters. The first, or incubational phase, covers the years leading up to the writing of the earliest draft in 1597-98. It would also include the composition of materials separately conceived and later interpolated, like the captain's narrative and some poetry, including Grisóstomo's "Song of Despair." The first and second phases belong to the Andalusian period of Cervantes' life, centered in Seville. The most disappointing period of his life, for its blighted hopes, it was the most amazing and prodigious for the literary projects conceived; life as observed and experienced had replaced, and temporarily shattered, the artful visions of romance.

According to my theory, the first phase closes when Cervantes takes up a story in a style wry with internal allusions, "burlas y donaires":

En un lugar de la Mancha, de cuyo nombre no quiero acordarme ... [11]

SECOND PHASE: GENESIS

The second phase is the genesis of the work as we know it, up to at least Chapter 8, the battle with the biscayan, and perhaps more. [12] The *Interlude of the Ballads,* a source for the parodies in Chapter 5, most likely dates from 1597. [13] The scrutiny of the books almost certainly was composed before 1599, [14] though it may have undergone elaboration later. I can see in this phase an alignment of episodes for the second sally taking shape from the adventure of the windmills, then of two monks and the biscayan (Chapter 8) to the adventure with the yanguesian carriers (Chapter 15).

This phase probes and outlines the exemplary plan. But if the author presses on in the fervor of experiment, and the knight and squire in expectation of illusions quickly to be granted, the forecast of the needful cure for the hidalgo's madness, like the inevitable return to the village, hangs over their prospects. The first sally ends with a recuperative stay in bed. The second will run its course to a similar end.

At its outset we have an exposure of illusions so ludicrous they may not survive even a day's experience. This day's literary duration is dependent, in one sense, on their hardiness; in another, on the author's resources for depicting them inwardly. For this he will draw on motifs from the parodied romances: "la ínsula," "el bálsamo de Fierabrás," "el yelmo de Mambrino," in this order; his scene will be a parodic adventure of chivalry; but his technique that draws the essentials to their full will be dialogue. Sancho's very first words are about the island: "—I pray you, have care, good sir knight, that you forget not that government of the island which you have promised me, for I shall be able to govern it were it never so great." Don Quijote's reply is a promise to deliver it.

Having put them on the road at dawn, the author's project is a day's course of adventures, each prefigured by a dialogue, and connected by a seemingly improvised chain of cause and effect. On the morning of the first day Don Quijote charges a windmill-giant, whose Briarean sails break his lance into shreds. And then the fall from Rocinante is so bruising he cannot attempt any more adventures this day. The pair make their way toward Puerto Lápice and spend the night in a wood, where Don Quijote improvises a new lance, using a branch: a day's literary duration in the summer of exemplary narrative.

If my conjecture is correct, this outing lasting two days originally consisted of three adventures: (1) windmills, (2) two friars of San Benito and biscayan, and (3) the yanguesians. [15] The second took place before noon of the second day; then Don Quijote and Sancho would stop to rest in mid-afternoon in the valley where the mares were feeding. Rocinante would then bring on a dismal turn of affairs, and the pair would seek to treat their sore members at an inn, where they would spend the night. If my conjecture is correct the original story did not go beyond this point. It depicted a course of adventures for Don Quijote lasting but two days on a scale that, however similar in details to the chivalric narratives, was a radical departure for its fulness. Two days on this life-size scale, with their bruises, cuts, and thrashings, would contrast with the limitless periods of adventures of mythical heroes like Amadís.

Having set down a story of short duration, did Cervantes let it lie incomplete? And for a long interval, say, two years or more? Or for so long an interval that a new start was in order? All speculation on this is at best a tribute to the truth we may never possess. In any case, the literary duration of the second sally to Chapter 8, the battle with the biscayan and the close of the original "First Part," is but a day and a half. Before the second day and its night could draw to a close Cervantes introduced a new combination of the pastoral and the chivalric, and pressed his story onto a new stage of development.

PASTORAL INTERLUDE

At the close of Chapter 8, the battle between Don Quijote and the biscayan is interrupted at a climactic point. The narrator, who will now identify himself as a "second author," confesses that his sources do not permit him to continue, brings the chapter to an abrupt close, but promises to satisfy his readers forthwith. The next chapter is the first of a "Second Part." This "Second Part" includes six chapters, 9 to 14. Chapter 9 opens with an account of the timely discovery by him in Toledo of a version of the Arabic original by Cide Hamete Benengeli. The heading for Chapter 10 reads: "De lo que más le avino a don Quijote con el vizcaíno, y del peligro en que se vio con una turba de yangüeses." "*Of the outcome of Don Quijote's battle with the biscayan, and of the dangers he faced with a mob of yanguesans."* [16] The adventure of the yanguesans is not recounted here, but in Chapter 15, and begins the "Third Part." Chapter 10 is a dialogue between knight and squire, and presumably preempts the afternoon hours of this day. At the close of the dialogue night falls, and the pair, unable to reach a village or inn, come upon some goatherds and spend the night with them. For almost a day, or until noon of the following, the strictly chivalric account is suspended, and we have an episode of pastoral themes.

Thus the "Second Part" introduces three changes or innovations.

(1) The stylistic parody of chivalric adventures is formalized into a mock history, but one provided by a combination of authors and texts. Henceforth the primitive threads of an exemplary account of the first and second phases become entwined with those of a parody of a chivalric history reinterpreted in "modern Castilian" from the Arabic original.

(2) The sequence of adventures for knight and squire is interrupted by an interlude of "rustic" goatherds and "feigned" shepherds. This episode of Grisóstomo and Marcela is as much a parallel to the main sequence and action as it is an interpolation.

(3) Within the parody, and the pastoral interlude providing variation in theme, style, and characters, the primitive plan of the exemplary story is notably expanded, and the prospect announces a book of major proportions.

We may speak of composition in a broad sense and include the revisions and recasting of portions in draft form, and even the changes an author is constantly making in his mind or on paper. It seems to me that in working out his story Cervantes reached two or three turning points. One of them, the most decisive, found him recasting a draft nearly complete as an exemplary story into the initial episodes of an extended parody. There is reason to suppose that at this point he imposed a division into Chapters and Parts on a story that, like his *Exemplary Novels,* did not have any, recasting and inserting whole sections and also revising the wording here and there, to fit the larger design.

I would guess that Cervantes reached this point about the year 1600. Perhaps by this year he had aligned in his mind or on paper the series of adventures taking Don Quijote from the inn of Juan Palomeque (Chapter 17), the battle with the sheep herds to the freeing of the galley slaves (Chapter 22) and retreat into Sierra Morena. In any case, in terms of his narrative, the first two important turning points were the decision to recast the earlier portions to fit a later and more elaborate idea, and the decision to incorporate "extraneous" materials already composed or in the process. Perhaps the two decisions were one and the same, perhaps not. In any case, what I have hypothesized as phases three and four are marked off from phase two on the one hand by these decisions and from phase five by another almost as important, as I shall explain presently.

The "Second Part," with its pastoral interlude, is then a new start, a new combination and a new outlook. These are facts in the book, apparent to any reader. We may first consider what clues literary history and biography furnish for explaining this new departure.

Two events of importance in the years 1599 and 1600, one literary and the other biographic, have recently been brought to bear on what we knew of the book's formative stages. In 1599 there was published in Madrid the First Part of Mateo Alemán's *El pícaro Guzmán de Alfarache*. The book appeared in March, or thereabouts, though the Royal License was granted in February 1598. Its success was immediate; its novelty irresistible: twelve editions of it appeared in two years, 1599 and 1600, a performance and a record that even *Don Quijote* never attained. [17] Scholars have for long assumed a relation, contrasts and parallels, between the two books, but in 1966 Américo Castro advanced certain arguments that magnify Alemán's influence on Cervantes. [18] These arguments imply that Cervantes' characters were conceived from the

beginning as a reaction, or a "tacit polemic," against Alemán's. One may disagree with this notion, while favoring
Castro's advocacy of a major role for Alemán's *Pícaro* in the
unfolding of themes and styles of narrative in *Don Quijote*.
Equally refreshing, the observations by Marcos A. Morínigo
on Cervantes' literary purposes clarify just where Alemán's
success with a new type of fiction would encourage him to
press on toward a similar goal. [19] There are good grounds for
speculating that Cervantes undertook to rival Alemán's success
in new prose fiction by continuing and enlarging the story
about his Manchegan hidalgo already in draft form, that is,
as he appears in the chapters of "Part One." In his *Pícaro*
Alemán provided an extensive, prototypal work of fascinating
interest for its morality, in excellent prose; its assortment of
interspersed tales and episodes had a new, hard craftiness,
nearly as distant from picaresque antecedents as *Don Quijote*
from chivalric romances. Cervantes undoubtedly read it with
vehement interest, and recalled specific details, yet he alluded
to it only once obliquely in *Don Quijote*, in the adventure
of the galley slaves (I. 22). Alemán distributed his autobiographical account into Parts and divided them into Books
and Chapters; at the close of Book One of his First Part he
introduced the amatory tale of byzantine flavor, "Ozmín y
Daraja."

Cervantes left Seville for an extended period in 1599; in
July of the next year, according to his most recent biographer,
Luis Astrana Marín, he moved away permanently. Hence the
year 1600 marks the end of the Sevillian or Andalusian period
of his life. There followed brief stays in various places in
New Castile: Toledo, Esquivias, Madrid, in the years 1600-
1602. [20] The passage in Chapter 9 describing the discovery of
scrolls or notebook containing Cide Hamete's history may be
in the way of an allusion to his stay in Toledo in 1601; perhaps
even to this phase of the enlargement, reconsideration, and
realignment of his story. We can even speculate that as the
episode of Grisóstomo and Marcela is a recreation of pastoral
romances, it could have been inspired by a return to the

region where fifteen years before *Galatea* had come forth. Had not Toledo and its vicinity been a traditional setting and even inspiration for bucolic themes since Garcilaso?

Does the pastoral interlude represent a third phase, or is it part of a later phase? It has been argued that at one stage of composition it formed part of the adventures taking place in Sierra Morena and appeared at the beginning of what is now Chapter 25. [21] According to these arguments, it was moved forward at the time of revising that also saw the division into Parts and Chapters. I shall give my own views on this question presently. For now we may consider in what ways this pastoral episode may appear decisive in the unfolding of Cervantes' story.

In it Cervantes introduces the serious literary treatment of contemporary life and sentiments, in a work already under way as a burlesque parody of archaic chivalry. Don Quijote alone has taken his calling seriously; but that calling is an aberration of his psychosis. Now Cervantes resolves to explore the inner recesses of his mind and his motives on a level of social expression and behavior impossible with Sancho. In a masterly stroke he conceives Don Quijote's discourse on the golden age, at once a dithyrambic unfolding of the exalted mind of a madman (in a period of lucid coherence) and a poetic equation, an interdependence, of the bucolic and chivalric life-styles. The tone in the exposition of the erotic in the discourse prefigures the despair and death of Grisóstomo. The poetic atoms swirling about in Don Quijote's declamations trace the depth of an inward need. Death is a cure to despair of love, but Grisóstomo's example is violent, too cruel to produce the kindred effect that Cardenio, another madman, will produce on the hidalgo's sensibilities. Cervantes has perceived the possibilities for characterization of his hidalgo that encounter with other men of feeling and imagination, with other lives in turmoil and anguish, will elicit. He grasps the possibilities this "new" knighthood for his hidalgo holds for externalizing the recesses of inner life, for unfolding the "psychology" of his characters. In the other direction he discerns the shapes of ensuing adventures and encounters with social reality as a strategic organization of episodes and plots. With an exemplary plan laid out Cervantes will attempt to bring forth an extended picture of contemporary life employing, in narrative prose, resources of drama and the epic.

Did Cervantes decide to interrupt Don Quijote's two days of adventures with this pastoral episode before or after he visualized the course of adventures leading up to the Cardenio episode in Sierra Morena (on the one hand) and (on the other) the enlargement of his parody into Parts? I am inclined to believe that he hit upon combining the pastoral and chivalric very early in the process of composition, but that he did not see in the first instance what possibilities were in store for him in such a combination. The Grisóstomo-Marcela interlude is conceived so completely as part of an unfolding that I propose we think of it as representing a complete phase.

Supposing Cervantes had first thought to introduce it as part of the story of the first night Don Quijote and Sancho spend in Sierra Morena. We should then have two episodes of "interrelated lives," Grisóstomo-Marcela and Cardenio-Luscinda, together and nearly breaking the sequence of Don Quijote's adventures. Is it not apparent that the decision to bring the episode forward entails also an idea for merging the chivalric and pastoral themes that vastly improves its place in the story and likewise enhances its possibilities in a novelistic art?

The reader, on contemplating the ensuing intermingling of lives that Cervantes now undertakes, may ask himself why, at this juncture, a counterpoint of pastoral and chivalric themes has thus challenged the novelist. The literary substance of both is romance, yet Cervantes has fixed his vision on the emergence of character. Neither Grisóstomo nor Marcela survives the episode as "feigned" shepherds, for they are real and/or contemporary figures, belonging to a given social class, and endowed with a reality of personal illusion that renders them parallels to the inspired hidalgo. A secret affinity between Grisóstomo's dark deed and Marcela's complete self-possession and the hidalgo's profession is surely latent in the outcome for him of those adventures immediately forthcoming, where he is proved ineffectual as knight-errant, in contrast to the adventure immediately preceding, where he attacks and in fact defeats a virile adversary, the biscayan. The affinity between the pastoral episode and the ensuing ones is the interaction of "lives in the making," but here Don Quijote and Sancho are only observers. It is as if Cervantes, after bringing to a close the battle with the biscayan, had reached out for a formula for continuing, and perceived that Don Quijote would be henceforth ineffectual as hero-knight, that the sum-total of his achievement would be a psychological conviction turned inward as a personalized moral affirmation.

I would say then, as conjecture, that Cervantes arrived at a major turning point in the years 1600-1601, and that the episode narrated in his "Second Part," Chapters 9-14, represents a decisive stage in the elaboration — enlargement and recasting — of his story, whether the final form of the episode as we know it was composed or recast in this period or later.

Now, for Cervantes, the focal point of the pastoral is the poetic vision that it lends to erotic emotion and stress. The episode is centered around the burial of a shepherd who has died of "the tyranny of love." Its gravamen is the poem we hear read at the burial, "Desperate Lover's Song," the last of the many poems by Grisóstomo. The contents of the poem so differ from the prose narrative surrounding it as to the cause of his death, it is apparent that Cervantes interpolated into his story a lover's lament in verse already composed. The poem, written perhaps five years previously (around 1595-97), belongs to the first phase of composition. To put it simply: the verses are as clear an expression as we need to tell us the shepherd died by suicide, by hanging:

> Y con esta opinión y un duro lazo,
> acelerando el miserable plazo
> a que me han conducido sus desdenes.

> ofreceré a los vientos cuerpo y alma,
> sin lauro o palma de futuros bienes.   I. 14

> *And with a hard knot and this strange opinion*
> *I will accelerate the wretched summon*
> *To which guided I am by her scorns rife,*
> *And offer to the air body and soul,*
> *Without hope or reward of future life.*

Yet the remarks about the poem in the prose narrative, and other remarks about his death "... y se murmura que ha muerto de amores de aquella endiablada moza de Marcela ..." "... *and they murmur that he died for love of that devilish lass Marcela* ..." (I. 12), confuse this very point. The *verse* discloses death by suicide, the *prose narrative* recasts the shepherd's motives with enigmatic inferences.

The discrepancies have puzzled more than one critic. [22] I submit they are due to the fact that Cervantes, having in mind an episode on a "Canción desesperada" already composed, where the disdained lover has committed suicide, pursued a quite different line of narrative (i.e., one of characterization) because he had now envisioned Grisóstomo and Marcela in terms of prose narrative. It is Marcela's cold reply to his passion that has driven him to suicide; yet the poem accuses her of inciting jealousy, of deceit as well as disdain, and even of inconstancy: "celos, ponedme un hierro en estas manos! / Dame, desdén, una torcida soga." Marcela's defense of her freedom and choice to remain chaste are the results of a reconsideration of unrequited love on Cervantes' part, and the whole is precisely his novelty in a treatment of pastoral themes in prose.

FOURTH PHASE

The opening Chapter of "Part Three," beginning "The wise Cide Hamete Benengeli recounteth that, as soon as Don Quijote had taken leave of the goatherds ... ," narrates the adventure with the yanguesian carriers. The ensuing episodes, comprising the "core" of adventures in the first summer, the contents of Chapters 15 to 27, will provide the occasions for Don Quijote to test his imagination against the facts of reality. One adventure connects with and develops into the next according to an exemplary delineation: the bruises inflicted by the yanguesian carriers call for an application of plasters, at the inn of Juan Palomeque el Zurdo; thereon follow the battles in the dark with the mule driver and Maritornes, and the concoction of the balsam of Fierabrás, and Sancho tossed in the blanket the next morning; then battle with the sheep flocks, and more blows and bruises; the adventures of the dead body and of the fulling mills by night; the winning of Mambrino's helmet the next morning and the freeing of the galley slaves at about 10 o'clock in the morning; [23] thereon retreat into the wilds of Sierra Morena, Cardenio's narrative, and Don Quijote's penance. Sancho then sets off for El Toboso and meets the priest and barber while passing the inn, and the three return to look for the hidalgo.

This sequence takes place in the course of three (or four) [24] nights and four (or five) days, according to the most discreet tally; towards its close, in Chapter 25, we meet with the date "twenty-second of August." Chapter 28 begins the "Fourth Part" and belongs to the fifth and final phase of composition.

Our phases thus follow Cervantes' division of his narrative into "Four Parts," as published in 1604-05. One could lay emphasis on the importance of this division for Cervantes. He abandoned it tacitly ten years later when he entitled the sequel "*Segunda Parte del ingenioso caballero . . . ,*" but in 1604 it probably exemplified for him the import of both structural and formal planning. In the adventures of the "Third Part" he deployed his episodes along a line of unfolding of his hero's imaginative excesses, and with a thrust and variation it would seem inconceivable that he could retrace or repeat any part of the design. The next phase, our fifth, was to be marked by elaborate schemes and techniques of interpolation; for, the hidalgo's obsessions having been played out in the exemplary sense, the incitement for adventures was diminished.

If the composition of the "Second Part" in our third phase is assignable to various months of the year 1601, one may also entertain, as an acceptable postulate, that the composition of the "central core" of episodes in the "Third Part" took place in the year 1602. Hence the date "twenty-second of August of this present year" (I. 25) may well refer to the year 1602, though 1603 cannot be discounted. The entire narrative was surely finished before Cervantes established a permanent or prolonged residence in Valladolid (where Philip III had removed his court in 1601), that is, before the spring of 1604. [25]

The hidalgo's exploits are aligned along an exclusive thread of narrative up to the time of his encounter with Cardenio. If one were to single out a given episode as the turning point in his fortunes and adventures, it would be this face-to-face encounter with a kindred and picturesquely alienated character. Don Quijote produces a stark, erratic impression on Cardenio, wherein the young man perceives a subconscious reflection of his derangement. Cardenio's impression on Don Quijote is even stronger, for it penetrates his distraught psyche from at least two directions. Don Quijote first sees in him a disdained lover driven to madness by grief, a tortured, paranymous spirit. And his sympathy extends to the search for a possible cure to his grief:

> —Los [buenos deseos] que yo tengo son de serviros; tanto, que tenía determinado de no salir destas sierras hasta hallaros y saber de vos si el dolor que en la estrañeza de vuestra vida mostráis tener se podía hallar algún género de remedio; y si fuera menester buscarle, buscarle con la diligencia posible. I. 24

> —*So great is mine affection to serve you, as I was fully resolved never to depart out of these mountains until I had found you, and known of yourself whether there might be any kind of remedy found for the grief that this your so unusual a kind of life argues doth possess your soul; and, if it were requisite, to search it out with all possible diligence.*

Upon entering them, the mountainous solitudes had brought to memory the marvellous adventures of his knightly models in similar surroundings. Hence the sight of Cardenio in rags, leaping from rock to rock, becomes a subconscious instigation to perform the penance of a disdained and distraught lover. But it will be the furious outplay of a feigned, that is, a rationalized, madness, with the result that it effects a release of his psychotic turbulence, so that a period of convalescence is in order. The fortuitous penance is consequently an outlet for his deranged senses and also the penitential but restorative period of a conditional "cure." Now the intrigue woven into the exemplary plot becomes the improvised efforts to bring the hidalgo back to his village.

The Cardenio episode, together with his narrative, was an essay or experiment in the variation and enlargement of kindred themes; its unity is the unfolding of Cardenio's character, alongside allegations of Don Fernando's treachery and Luscinda's frailty. Correspondingly, Dorotea's narrative and character will supply a similar unity to the episodes of the "Fourth Part" when she intervenes with Cardenio in Don Quijote's adventures. If Cardenio's madness serves as catalyst for Don Quijote's "cure," her entreaty as Princess Micomicona works as a stratagem to induce the knight to take the way home. Phase four is on one level the "essay of cure" and on another an advance in the design of intercalated narratives. The lives of characters interact, as in the case of Cardenio's and Don Quijote's, and we have "intercalated lives," so to speak, rather than intercalated plots or tales. The next advance and the next phase is signaled by the appearance of Dorotea.

My premise is, therefore, that the Cardenio episode represents the first of two stages in sentimental narrative involving two pairs of lovers, in this fourth phase, and in the period 1602-03. Having pursued a narrative thread of adventures for his hidalgo over a period of about five years, from 1597 to 1602, Cervantes was now drawn irresistibly to the narrative of amatory psychology and to sentimental romance, and chose to extend the hidalgo's "history" with variations on these. As a consequence the course of mock chivalric adventures is all but brought to a standstill; yet this state of affairs invites the ensuing exploration of Don Quijote's psychological world: enchantments, real or imagined.

FIFTH PHASE [Chapters 28-52]

> *Most happy and fortunate were those times wherein the thrice audacious and bold knight, Don Quijote of the Mancha, was bestowed on the world, by whose most honourable resolution to revive and renew in it the already worn-out and well-nigh deceased exercise of arms, we joy in this, our so niggard and scant an age of all pastimes, not only the sweetness of his true history, but also of the other tales and digressions contained therein, which are in some respects no less pleasing, artificial, and true than the very history itself; the which, prosecuting the carded, spun, and self-twined thread of the relation, says that, as the curate began to bethink himself upon some answer that might both comfort and animate Cardenio, he was hindered by a voice which came to his hearing, said very dolefully the words ensuing:*
>
> *—O God! is it possible that I have yet found out the place which may serve for a hidden sepulchre to the load of this loathsome body that I unwillingly bear so long? I. 28*

The opening passage of the "Fourth Part" expresses perfectly the conception Cervantes has worked toward. The point of convergence for Don Quijote's history and the stories of intercalated lives is romantic incident. On this day (the twenty-ninth of the action by Ríos' count) we hear the second portion of Cardenio's narrative, then Dorotea's; then we have (in Cuesta's second edition) a fleeting view of Ginés de Pasamonte, and a reappearance of Andresillo. On the next day, after arrival at the inn, we hear a reading of "The Curious Impertinent," while Don Quijote slays the giant in his sleep; at its close we meet Don Fernando and Luscinda, and witness the happy outcome of their trials; later that afternoon there arrive at the inn the captain Ruy Pérez and Zoraida, and after supper and Don Quijote's discourse on arms and letters we hear their story; then, that same evening, the captain's brother, Juan Pérez, and his daughter, Doña Clara, arrive; after a second supper [26] there follows the unwonted coincidence and scene of their reunion; that night Don Quijote guards the castle-inn, and a little before dawn Don Luis, disguised as a horse-boy, awakens the guests, singing the ballad "Love's Shipman." These are by far the longest twenty-four-hour periods of literary duration in the entire story. It appears that Cervantes endeavored virtuoso-like to give this diversity of lives and fictions, coincidence and reunions, a simple unity of time and place. His audacity here ranges further than his originality, in weaving symmetrical strands of narrative and plot together, because that unity is at once the synthesis of the techniques of a novelist and a dramatist.

Love and marriage are themes treated particularly in each of the stories. The Dorotea-Don Fernando intrigue is the most original, complete, and refined, psychologically. One may assume this is so because it was put to paper in this the fifth phase. In Dorotea's narrative in Chapter 28 we find details introduced almost certainly from the chivalric romance published in 1602, *Don Policisne de Boecia.* [27] The earliest of the stories is the captain's narrative, written in part as early as 1589. Coming between these two, "The Curious Impertinent" belongs to either the third or fourth phase. We ought, however, to distinguish between the time of composition of this Italianate novel and the time of its interpolation in Don Quijote's history. The latter belongs to this fifth phase, and clearly reflects Cervantes' preoccupation with alignment and variation of themes. It is significant that the only break in the reading of it is the episode of the wine-skins, with its mock battle and gushing of blood. The reading is introduced by a lively commentary on the fictions of chivalry, and their appeal to individual tastes. And it is the curate, holding views similar to Cervantes' on literary topics, who reads the novel to his audience and also supplies at its close an inimitable judgment on it. In the case of the other stories the focus on the characters' lives in the making is the relation between the past narratives of Cardenio and Dorotea, and then the appearance of Don Fernando and Luscinda, and the present exemplary plot of Don Quijote's adventures. "The Curious

Impertinent" is the only literary or composed fiction introduced, and for this reason appears decidedly "extraneous."
Yet the workings of its psychological themes are comple-
mentary to the others; unlike them, it ends in disillusion and
disaster, for it is a Cervantic treatment of love and marriage
from the thither side of wedlock, whereas the prospects for
the four reunited couples in the inn are cloudless. The literary
duration of this reading has little to do with verisimilitude,
but by suspending entirely one fiction for the interval (the
afternoon hours of the siesta) of the performed reading of
another, Cervantes extracted a measure of substance for the
time and place of his group of listeners from a convention
little modified over the centuries by a plethora of storytellers.
Moreover, contrary to that convention, he did not repeat his
own elaborate device, but straightway set out to exceed it.

STORY OF THE CAPTIVE CAPTAIN

The narratives of Cardenio and Dorotea take us back into
events only recently accomplished and then played out in
our presence to their sentimental resolution; they provide a
marginal picture of relations between classes and individuals
that can only be thought of as contemporaneous with Spanish
society in the years of their composition, ca. 1600. The captain's narrative, on the other hand, takes his hearers, individuals from that very society, back into an historical past
and to an experience known to few Spaniards relatively. His
very dress and the picture he forms with the woman who
accompanies him betoken a strangeness ensuing as much
from a remoteness in time as of place and customs. When we
have heard his story we know that it reaches back into an
historical past that remains distant in order to create a span
of time and experience between a far-off point and this present
scene of its telling and outcome. Now that point is actually
further removed from this moment than the historical dates
he mentions, for in describing his family origin and separation
from his father and brothers the captain's account virtually

recedes out of the focus of history and autobiography into folklore and myth.

A folk motif and a legend — the separation of sons from their father, and the division of his wealth by the father — are precisely the opening strands of narrative. It seems that Cervantes, having made the decision to enjoin to Don Quijote's adventures the telling of a story written some ten years previously, considered this historical tale as a tale principally. That is, he sought for his point of departure (the folk element of sons separated from their father) the corresponding resolution: their long-awaited reunion, with the elements of surprise and recognition.

When looked at in its overall movement and details, the episode and narrative of the captain will disclose these constituents: (1) a story of separation and eventual reunion of brothers and father; (2) a story, for the captive, of liberation and escape, and for Zoraida of fulfilment of an ideal to embrace the Christian faith; (3) a narrative of historical events in the naval and military past of Spain and an account of Spanish captives in Turkey and Algiers. These constituents, moreover, appear as combinations of other subordinate elements, superimposed so as to form a single but stratified structure.

Of these the earliest by date of composition is the portion of the story in Chapter 39 up to the point where mention is made of Don Pedro de Aguilar. There we learn that one of Don Fernando's companions is the brother of Don Pedro. The close of the Chapter, and the insertion of the two sonnets attributed to Don Pedro, are part of the present dramatic scene and belong to the interpolation scheme of phase five. Now, few of Cervantes' narratives betray their skeletal outlines so entirely as this first portion and the ensuing second portion of Chapter 40. He begins by elaborating a folk motif, within the dim outlines of an exemplary story (the father's prodigality); then, precisely at the point where we hear "This will be the twenty-second year since I left my father's house...", he takes up a narrative of travel and soldiering, a military

memoir, where the thread becomes an exact account of places
and dates, year by year, 1567 to 1571 — the year of Lepan-
to and for him of captivity; then "I was the year ensuing of
1572 in Navarino . . . We returned to Constantinople, and the
next year after, being that of '73, we learned how Don Juan
had gained Tunis . . ." There follows a detailed account of
the attack on the Goleta and its loss to the Turks (on August
23, 1574). He gives a full account of the siege of the Goleta,
but no event after 1574 is mentioned or described. In fact,
the next fifteen years of captivity (up to the day Zoraida's
reed and cloth appeared) are described as largely uneventful,
except for the change of masters and the journey from Constantinople to Algiers.

Numerous attempts at escape failed, and liberty seemed
an impossible dream, yet no single day in those years of
captivity is memorable: but in that span of time Ruy Pérez
turned from a youth of twenty-five to the mature man of
forty-one.

The arrival at Algiers and prison life in the bagnio under
the cruel Azán Agá (i.e., Hasan Bāšā) are described with no
reference to the passage of years; but the division between
this portion of the story and the description of the bagnio on
the day Zoraida's reed and cloth first appeared is made by the
passage on "the Spanish soldier Saavedra." All revelations
up to this point are preliminary to the story of escape with
Zoraida, and this escape and the scenes in her father's garden
and at sea have taken place in the months, nay, the weeks and
days immediately preceding.

It is evident that Cervantes wished to build his story of
fabulous escape and idealization of Zoraida on the elements
of the three preliminary portions, the folktale, the military
memoir, a captive's memoir, that is, the scenes in the bagnio. [28]
The thread of continuity between them is romantic alignment,
and up to now we know little of the captain's qualities of
character. I find this alignment rudimentary and evidence of
hesitant efforts for one embarking on a new course; evidence,
that is, of Cervantes' trial to find his own way as a novelist

in 1589-90. He was looking back to the gravest period of his life, and sought the meaning of his own captivity and liberation in lasting and ideal terms.

Such is his skill in weaving diverse strands into a romantic whole that one is seldom provoked into analyzing the given facts about Zoraida and the captain. On arrival at the inn Ruy Pérez appears in every respect a man of mature age and bearing, as befits his trials and experience; he "was of strong and comely making, of the age of forty years or thereabouts, ... such as, if he were well attired, men would take him to be a person of quality and good birth." (I. 37). From his story one must assume that when, twenty-two years ago, he left his father's house he had attained his eighteenth or nineteenth year. The year of his birth would be, therefore, 1547 or 1548. Cervantes' age, in 1589-90, was forty-two. The picture we form of Zoraida is that of a girl of great courage, passion, and intelligence; her beauty, the equal in radiance to Dorotea's and Luscinda's, is that of late adolescence, of chastity. This rare creature, from her point of vantage overlooking the bagnio, has observed for many months, and selected, from among the other Christian slaves to be her liberator and husband, a man nearly her father's age; or, what amounts to the same thing, a man twice her age, as a father substitute. Absorbed in events of that day, we fail to see that Cervantes is about to weave a fanciful love plot between an exotic and fervent girl and a forty-one-year-old soldier.

Yet we must desist from subjecting Cervantes' tale of love and liberation to analysis as if it were his exemplary novel of sentimental affinities and marriage; that is, as if the romantic story of 1589 were an exemplary story of 1603 or later. He was resolute in keeping intact, as first conceived, the ideal and exalted nature of his characters. Nor must we pursue beyond acceptance the truthfulness of and correspondence between the captain's ideal picture of Zoraida and the upward thrust of his own emotional constraint. Zoraida is the ideal of womanhood and heavenly emancipation for Ruy Pérez in flesh and desire as Dulcinea is for Don Quijote in desire alone. And the captain is an ideal of manhood worthy of Zoraida's entrusting of her life, fortune, and salvation. No reservations must intrude into our picture of them in the inn, thereby lessening the effect of their noble qualities and the magical effect of their story. Yet the captain's story is a veritable tale of heroic adventure adumbrating an entire mythical movement of the kind Don Quijote dreams of and aspires to, and the latter's frustrations, like his dreams, are made to look ridiculous, grotesque.

Artistically, the captive's story is a primitive piece of narrative by comparison with the exemplary course of Don Quijote's mock adventures. And, of course, in the interval of its recital or telling, the captain before us ceases to be this living but fictional character and becomes the storyteller conscious of his artifice, as he hints at on closing his tale. Such a resolution between present circumstance and past experience is not open to the hidalgo, who belongs to another order of fiction and characterization. We may find it a retrogression on the part of Cervantes to have brought his amatory plots to solution in the dewy scenes of exuberant tears, those tears that banish apparently all tribulations before any of the deepest needs and desires of these four pairs of lovers, but Cervantes was impelled by his own tastes and inclinations to retrieve as a romancer what he had expedited as exemplary analyst and moralist, and to recover in phase five what of poetic sentiment and narrative variety he had forgone in devising the chain of Don Quijote's adventure in the preceding phase.

The reunion of Ruy and Juan Pérez depends for dramatic effect on a separation of many years, and twenty-two years must have seemed sufficient to Cervantes as he brought forward onto the scale of the scenes at the inn a story conceived many years before. As a consequence, the present scene of reunion must be dated as of the year 1589, and the summer of this year the time of fortuitous meeting, liberation, and escape for the captive and Zoraida. But for other reasons the scene may be presumed to take place some twelve years later.

The stratified yet uninvolved structure of the captive's story tells us a great deal about Cervantes' means and ends in early efforts at exemplary narration. If the earlier phase bespeaks an unalloyed zest for accumulation of narrative elements and fortuitously turned plots, the later phase, our fifth, evinces pursuit of dramatic engagements out of these very elements so accumulated, when struck for theatrical effects. In the captive's narrative we go from one prodigious disclosure and turn of events to a final realization of the marvellous personages we have before us; immediately thereafter Juan Pérez arrives at the inn, and our tale and its fine personages move upward, to the finale of a third act, as it were, onto the scene of their dramatic recognition and reunion. The sentimental effect of tears, expertly aimed for, is thus dependent upon an immediate resolution of our tale by this little drama. Well aware of his means and ends, Cervantes could not forgo disclosing them, in the comments made by Don Fernando:

> —Por cierto, señor capitán, el modo con que habéis contado este estraño suceso ha sido tal, que iguala a la novedad y estrañeza del mesmo caso. Todo es peregrino, y raro, y lleno de accidentes que maravillan y suspenden a quien los oye; y es de tal manera el gusto que hemos recebido en escuchalle, que aunque nos hallara el día de mañana entretenidos en el mesmo cuento, holgáramos que de nuevo se comenzara. I. 42

> —Truly, captain, the manner wherewithal you have recounted this marvellous success hath been such as it may be paragoned to the novelty and strangeness of the event itself. And so great is the delight we have taken in the hearing thereof, as I do believe that although we had spent the time from hence till to-morrow in listening to it, yet should we be glad to hear it told over once again.

For Cervantes the "marvellous events" in Ruy Pérez' life recounted as a story or "history" converged with the account of Don Quijote's "unheard of" aberration and ingenuity. A period of "twenty-two years" reaching into the past was initially a purely narrative ingredient lending cogency to historical and autobiographical details, and might have served simply as an indefinite period in a story having no immediate relation to the present, like "The Curious Impertinent." But now (in our fifth phase) Cervantes was obliged to bring the unity of time of his episodes in the inn to rest upon it, thus aligning beyond Don Quijote's discourse on arms and letters and the captive's story the appearance of Juan Pérez de Viedma, and the ensuing episode of Doña Clara and Don Luis. In this way, then, the duration of "twenty-two years" within the tale was made to hold together the stratified structure of its constituents and to furnish the arrangement for surprise and marvellous coincidence in the reunion of brothers. This was no mechanical expedient, but an intuition of the esthetic unity between a literary duration within the captive's story and the "strange coincidence" it now effected in a fortuitous reunion:

> *Then did the captain draw near to embrace his brother; but he held him off a while with his arms, to note whether it was he or no; but when he once knew him, he embraced him so lovingly, and with such abundance of tears, as did attract the like from all the beholders. The words that the brothers spoke one to another, and the feeling affection which they showed, can hardly be conceived, and therefore much less written by any one whatsoever. I. 42*

NOVELTY AND THE NEW COMEDY

By the rule of logic and dates this scene takes place in the late hours of a night at the close of summer in the year 1589. In the captive's story this night king Philip II reigns over Spain's empire. The following day the uproar and fracas on Mambrino's basin-helmet ensue; these lead to a hoax-enchantment on the next day as a ploy for enducing the hidalgo to allow himself to be taken back to his village. With Don Quijote the mark of a ruse as extravagant as it is entertaining, Cervantes can expand the psychological fervor in an aberrant belief in enchantments and pursue an exemplary plot and parody as if it were comedy. This, the great innovation of phase five, became possible for him after 1600-1602, with the result that the departure from the inn of the entourage escorting Don Quijote homeward in the cart is envisioned by us as a scene in the year 1603; for the ensuing commentary by the curate and the canon of Toledo on Lope de Vega's plays, a calculated coupling of the old chivalric romances and the new comedy, relate to a state of affairs well into the reign of Philip III. [29] What we know of Cervantes' and Lope's relations with one another reveals they worsened in 1603-04. Yet from this time Cervantes was never again to feel intimidated by Lope's fame and success. An emboldened confidence in the great novelty of prose narrative that could compete with Lope's new comedy in variety, invention, and romantic interest is implicit where Cervantes provokes his characters to a reproof of Lope's charming demerits.

Phase five is a novelistic complexity of lives staged and resolved with techniques of comedy and its unities of time and place. If the inn is a stage for the novel of a contemporary world, that world is staged as a parody of the enchanted castles of Don Quijote's romances. Understanding this we see why Cervantes was impelled to consummate his exemplary plot with a fortuitous verisimilitude and unity of time. They followed as a consequence of the interaction between the storied lives of his secondary characters and the impulsive career of his mock knight.

Cervantes devised and attained to a novel of contemporary society by prefixing the unity of character of his exemplary narrative to the unity of time and place requisite in a dramatic but verisimilar plot. Of course the originality of *Don Quijote*, vis-à-vis Lope's *comedia*, did not lie in its spontaneous fusion of multiple plots and fictions, for here Cervantes had only unaffectedly overcome the pretensions and tastes of his age. Yet it is doubtful whether he could have provided psychological magnitude in a parody of chivalric adventure without a creative indagation into the lives of his creatures, each of them coming forth with a sentimental tale, acting out its outcome before a gathering, and moving from isolation and anxiety to social accommodation.

The interlaced resolutions of these stories tender, at their brightest, the happier prospects of marriage in accord with personal affinities sanctioned socially; a simple unity of time and place provides for a complexity of personal wills and desires, in a *comedia en prosa*, if you will. [30] The action, if accumulative and suspenseful in the theatrical sense, is that of a dramatic plot narrated, its delayed movement in the way of a redressing of analytic discourse for sentimental romance. The complete lack of dependence on the fictitious narrator, Cide Hamete, for these scenes is notable; the omniscience they demand is that of a playwright superintending techniques and casts, not the omniscience of an historian or epic poet, with exclusive right to embellish his hero's trajectory.

There is indeed an irreversible process at work in the movement of the "Fourth Part" from an engagement and resolution of these four amatory plots in forthcoming marriages to the ascendance of Don Quijote's aberration to the psychical quiddity of states of enchantment. The adventure of the Princess of Micomicona dissipates, to Sancho's despair, into a state of spellbound quiescence for his master. The hoax enchantment, with the absurd prophecy of marriage between Don Quijote and Dulcinea, evolves from the resolution of these four love plots, and enlists their entire casts, but its unfolding brings into view a mythical figuration for his renown as a mock knight. [31] Isolated in his delusion, while riding encaged in the cart, Don Quijote styles himself "a new knight in the world." In phase five the isolation of the mock hero within his psychosis has been completed by the cast of characters surrounding him. In the Second Part of 1615 the hidalgo will play out a psychological role in a world contrived to his illusion and fame.

The day spent in the company of the canon of Toledo and the day of arrival back in the village, a Sunday, are the last two days narrated in the summer of the First Part. [32]

Their incidents are a kind of reprise of the earlier fortuitous encounters of the second and third phases, and include pastoral themes in the tale of Eugenio and Leandra.

As brought to a finish in the spring of 1604 the book was a complete narrative in the sense that its characters were fully drawn and the plot played out to its temporal limits according to an exemplary plan. Don Quijote and Sancho had been gone from their village on a "sally" lasting but two weeks or so, the entire verisimilitude of time and location of their adventures resting on the outplay of the hidalgo's psychosomatic projections. When Cervantes took up the story again six or seven years later he had only to retrace this design of venturing forth and return within a "likely" time span.

A cure for the hidalgo that would see him regaining his sanity and renouncing his role as knight was implicit in a sequel, again, according to the exemplary plan of the original idea. In 1604 a complete cure at the close of the second sally was not extant, for a third sally lay in the offing. Yet the First Part did not close without foreboding for the eventual finality of the sequel. The valedictory poems celebrate a deceased whose deeds already encumber the archives of La Mancha. [33] Ten years later Cervantes, on closing the sequel, would affix to the death of Don Quijote his cure.

He had conceived the literary reality of his hidalgo, and the time and place of his narrative, in what we should call a narrative past, yet as he endowed him with qualities and characteristics he brought him and his story forth perdurably into the presence of an observer contemporaneous with the time of writing, the years 1597-1604. It was this talismanic affinity between the fictional reality of his character and the picture of the historical and social scene in his story that would create for Don Quijote a literary reality outside his book in the material world.

At the close of the First Part, then, Cervantes had come full circle in devising a mythical figuration for his mock hero, and I think this is the full and final novelty of his advance through our five phases. In the next phase the notoriety of his fictional character and his literary fame in the exterior world of Spanish society would begin to act upon the process of his delineation in the subjectivity of his creator.

In 1605 the character of "Don Quijote" and his age, "almost fifty," were definable within the existence of such an hidalgo in a recent past that carried forward onto a contemporary scene, and indeed onto the day of composition. But then this very scene, historical and contemporary, moved inexorably through the succession of years, from 1605 forward, and the permanence of that character would prove immune to the passage of time and events. The autonomy of Don Quijote prescribed this immunity. A figure of the imagination, yet embodied and, as it were, clothed with all manner of historical and social particularities, he transcended these and asserted the prerogatives of a mythical creature, comparable to Orlando and Amadís.

The public success of the First Part in the five years 1605 to 1610 [34] worked a direct influence on Cervantes' ideas for a sequel, subtly transferring the emphasis onto the mock mythical and romantic elements of his hero, and reducing the contrasts supporting an exemplary parody. With the publication of the First Part the image of the hidalgo as a mock knight was impressed triumphantly on the imagination of the great public. It was for the character of the hidalgo, and the mock role he assumed for himself and Sancho, that Cervantes' book became vividly fixed in the mind of his contemporaries. The book evoked a "real person" from an immediate reality and a poetic characterization from a literary mode. The character was identified by that public with his immediate circumstances, the mocking attempt to have adventures in the Spain of 1600. To a much lesser extent was the character identified with the story, its exemplary train and outcome, and the plot inscribing those adventures. Hence the time of the hidalgo as a "real" person faded into and merged with the time of the fictional knight as a parody. This ideal time and season of his adventures was prescribed, in the way of a conceit, by the romances his grotesque chivalry evoked: the fanciful spring and summer of his mythical figuration.

For Cervantes his fiction was focussed on the decisive moment of his hidalgo's existence, the transformation brought on by his diseased imagination and played out in the course of weeks and months in the final summer of that life time. His hidalgo's story was acted out within the course of a single summer; for this reason the sequel had to continue the story after an interval of "almost a month," unaffected by the solar course from summer to winter. But would this summer of the sequel be a prolongation of the first? Or would it begin it anew?

Throughout the sequel the adventures of the First Part, the penance in Sierra Morena, Sancho's blanketing, and his embassy to Dulcinea abide with the force and vivid effect of recent events. But by a continuation of another sort Cervantes will now move the social and contemporary scene of the story forward to the time of his public success with the First Part, so that historically the background in the Second Part will be Spain in the years 1610-1614. Within these two movements, one the time and duration of his exemplary narrative and a matter of months, and the other historical and a matter of years, he fixed the beginning of the sequel as the springtime of a new but indefinite year, its course of adventures forthcoming in incipient summer. The second summer is thus a continuation of the first in the sense of our exemplary plot and its prolongation as for the historical scene, but its mythical similitude and "recurrence," if so Joycean a term may be permitted, in the parodistic and mock-romantic sense.

The clue to this motion of "quixotic" times is of course the image Don Quijote has of himself as a knight. That image is a distortion of certain elements of time and character in the romances he emulates, and a poetic distortion. Cervantes projects him psychically into the time and place of his imagination as part of his parody, but while carrying out that parody the real and historical time and place of his experiences are absorbed as an "adventure" into that image of his hero. Hence Don Quijote's real and exemplary experiences take place in a poetic time and season of wish fulfilment inspired by his psychosis and likewise conform to his "living" fame in the exterior world.

The temporal movement of adventures in the second summer was to have three levels, exemplary, historical, and mythical. We can expect to find "consistency" in this motion on the level of the mythical, for Don Quijote's image of himself as mythical hero occupies the center and likewise traces the arc it describes on the horizon of the material world.

We shall therefore premise a "mythical plan" underlying the continuation of our exemplary plan and plot. This mythical plan, in the first instance, projected an itinerary with Zaragoza as its goal. The season would be late spring, arrival at the Aragonese capital to coincide with the feast day of Saint George in late April or early May, the time of the "famous jousts." But once under way the very nature of his materials would encourage Cervantes to enlarge and expand his narrative, introducing novel complexities that delayed progress towards Zaragoza. The mythical trajectory of his hero was necessarily an enlargement of his psychological evolution. The literary duration of both was the illusion of a perpetual late spring or early summer as the time and season of his mythical renown. But the initial plan was modified in 1614, with the substitution of Barcelona for Zaragoza and the feast day of Saint John's Nativity for the feast day of Saint George. As we shall see, the itinerary of the third sally is a tracing out of this mythical plan, for its goals, turns, and duration will reveal how the inner complexities of his psychological plot instigated Cervantes to delay progress toward and arrival at Zaragoza, until it was no longer feasible as a destination.

The itinerary is thus the main clue for determining the phases of composition in the sequel. [35] There were three. The first phase includes the preliminary scenes up to Chapter

7, departure in Chapter 8, and the course of adventures to arrival at the banks of the Ebro in Chapter 29. The direction of travel is first north to El Toboso and toward Zaragoza, but then veers east and then south again to the cave of Montesinos and the lakes of Ruidera, then north again toward the Ebro. The duration of this course according to Ríos was nineteen days and according to Hartzenbusch twenty-nine days. The season is vernal.

The second phase consists of the entire sojourn at the ducal palace, Chapters 30 to 58. And here the season is summer. Chapter 59, where Cervantes reveals direct knowledge of Avellaneda's imitation, introduces the third and final phase, and here the season is again vernal, as Don Quijote and Sancho travel toward Barcelona, and arrive there on midsummer eve.

Conception and composition of Chapters 1 to 7 and 8 to 29 in phase one falls into the period 1609-1613, of Chapters 30 to 58 in phase two in the summer of 1614, and of the final phase in the fall and winter months of 1614-15. [36]

Talk in the opening scenes on the menace of Turkish fleets to the coasts of Spain, and the notoriety of the arbitristas in the reign of Philip III, reveal a political, social, and military background impossible to detect in the book published in 1604-05. The year 1609 or 1610 seems most probable as the date of composition of these scenes in Chapters 1 to 7. [37] In the interval of five or six years Cervantes had devoted his efforts to the *Novelas ejemplares* and *Comedias y entremeses* published in 1613 and 1615 respectively. Within this interval the First Part had undergone seven or eight editions, and by Cervantes' own estimate Don Quijote's *historia* had appeared in more than twelve thousand printed tomes. This interval of five years is the prerequisite to facts as known to Sansón Carrasco, who comes forth to meet the knight with details of the published book:

> —Desa manera, ¿verdad es que hay historia mía, y que fue moro y sabio el que la compuso?

Es tan verdad, señor —dijo Sansón—, que tengo para mí que el día de hoy están impresos más de doce mil libros de la tal historia; si no, dígalo Portugal, Barcelona, y Valencia, donde se han impreso; y aun hay fama que se está imprimiendo en Amberes, y a mí se me trasluce que no ha de haber nación ni lengua donde no se traduzga. II. 3

—*Then it seems my history is extant, and that he was a Moor and a wise man that made it?*

—*So true it is, quoth Sansón —, that, upon my knowledge, at this day there be printed above twelve thousand copies of your history; if not, let Portugal, Barcelona, and Valencia speak, where they have been printed; and the report goes that they are now printing at Antwerp, and I have a kind of guess that there is no nation or language where they will not be translated.* [38]

"TE DOY A DON QUIJOTE DILATADO"

"I give thee Don Quijote enlarged," these words from the Prologue of 1615 underscore the design of enlargement of the hero's portrait and the prolongation of his career. And because the design continues the course of the first summer into the second, the enlargement and the prolongation are cast within the lapse and movement of an exemplary time. The story of that first summer now appears in a book; its episodes will presently intervene as a published history as well as those events memorable for Don Quijote and Sancho for their recentness.

After 1605 the prolongation of Don Quijote's mock chivalric career and the enlargement of his portrait were drawn from the exemplary plan of the First Part and projected forward onto the mythical plan of the third sally, the autonomy of the hero now commensurate with his mythical fame. The point of departure was reached by Cervantes most likely in the year 1610. By this year it seems he would have completed Chapters 1 through 7 and perhaps more. In the Prologue (completed before July 1612) to the *Exemplary Novels* he promised, among other works, the forthcoming Second Part to *Don Quijote*. Here we find a statement of the plan to enlarge and expand: "... y primero verás, y con brevedad, dilatadas las hazañas de don Quijote y donaires de Sancho Panza ..." A similar wording appears in the opening passage of Chapter 8:

"¡Bendito sea el poderoso Alá! —dice Hamete Benengeli al comienzo deste octavo capítulo—. ¡Bendito sea Alá!" repite tres veces, y dice que da estas bendiciones por ver que tiene ya en compaña a don Quijote y a Sancho, y que los letores de su agradable historia pueden hacer cuenta que *desde este punto comienzan las hazañas y donaires de don Quijote y de su escudero.*

An enlargement and expansion of Don Quijote's deeds as a plan would call for a temporal interval of indefinite duration. As Cervantes composed, through the years 1612, 1613, and 1614, the new course of adventures, adding, expanding, or dilating, he delayed arrival at Zaragoza, as exemplified in the round-about itinerary. Although adventures followed in sequence from El Toboso to the banks of the Ebro, temporal succession would leave the solar season and its landscape essentially unaffected, and the vernal season was prolonged for as long as his characters delayed their arrival at Zaragoza. That Cervantes believed he had carried out his declared aim is evident in the Prologue of 1615 where he insists on the finality of the outcome for Don Quijote. Having drawn out his hidalgo-hero to this magnitude, any comparison with the perfidious character of Avellaneda's travesty was infamous:

... consideres que esta *segunda parte de Don Quijote* que te ofrezco es cortada del mismo artífice y del mesmo paño que la primera, y que en ella te doy a don Quijote dilatado, y, finalmente, muerto y sepultado, porque ninguno se atreva a levantarle nuevos testimonios ... *Prólogo,* 1615.

... *consider that this* second part of Don Quijote, *which I offer thee, is framed by the same art and cut out of the same cloth that the first was. In it I present thee with Don Quijote enlarged, and at last dead and buried, and so no man presume to raise any further reports of him ...*

The enlargement of the hero-knight brought into alignment the three temporal movements that had unified his story from the time of the "Fourth Part," — the exemplary, the

mock chivalric or romantic, and the historical. The wonder of
Cervantes' invention — and our scheme of three movements
is nothing more than an approach to it — is that the psychological delineation of his mock knight and squire deepened
and clarified progressively as he moved the scene and time
of his fiction forward with the historical scene of the years of
its composition. Don Quijote had for him an "actuality" of a
mythical being embodied in the real world. The fiction of his
"knighthood' had been established as a fact in historical time.
In Chapter 16, three or four days after departure from their
village, Don Quijote and Sancho meet the Knight of the
Green Coat, Don Diego de Miranda. This stranger, so
elegantly dressed as to accent a festive accord with the
season of spring, provokes from Don Quijote an avowal of
his knighthood, a self-profession.

> Quise resucitar la ya muerta andante caballería, y ha muchos
> días que, tropezando aquí, cayendo allí, despeñándome acá y levan-
> tándome acullá, he cumplido gran parte de mi deseo, socorriendo
> viudas, amparando doncellas y favoreciendo casadas, huérfanos y
> pupilos, propio y natural oficio de caballeros andantes; y así, por
> mis valerosas, muchas y cristianas hazañas he merecido andar ya
> en estampa en casi todas o las más naciones del mundo. Treinta
> mil volúmenes se han impreso de mi historia, y lleva camino de
> imprimirse treinta mil veces de millares, si el cielo no lo remedia.
> II. 16

According to our exemplary duration only a week or so
has passed since the knight, through Sansón Carrasco, discovered that a history of his first two sallies had appeared
in print. Sanson spoke of *twelve thousand* copies. Here it is
the knight himself who speaks of that printed history and
of the fame that accrues to him through his deeds. Not
twelve thousand copies, but *thirty* thousand copies, and then
thirty thousand times thirty thousand. [39]

It was in September or October of 1614 that Cervantes
first saw a printed copy of Avellaneda's travesty, with its
scurrilous prologue. The scene in the inn in Chapter 59 was
in the way of a first reaction; the Prologue of 1615 is a more

meditated rebuttal. Avellaneda's book had been approved
(assuming that the official notices are genuine) by ecclesiastical
authority in Tarragona, Aragón, on April 18, 1614, and li-
censed for printing on July 4, and probably offered for sale
the next month. [40] One must suppose that it was completed
early in 1614, and that Cervantes, though he may have had
some notice of it, did not know its contents until he saw
the printed copy that came into his hands after he had
composed the departure of Don Quijote and Sancho from
the ducal palace. [41] From this point in the story the usurper
was to have an unforeseen effect. Having delayed arrival at
Zaragoza, having delayed bringing the course of adventures
to its announced goal and the close of his story, Cervantes
was provoked by his imitator to alter his hero's course and
to end his story with a deliberated discredit of the false
author.

The story in Chapters 59 to the end, in our third phase,
completed in an unforeseen way the delineation of the hero.
The apocryphal version was given a reality in the story, and
consequently Don Quijote's mythical delineation was completed by the historical scene of 1614-1615.

The change in itinerary became the fortuitous instigation
to complete the original plan with Barcelona as the final goal.
When asked by Don Juan and Don Jerónimo, in the scene
in the inn, "whither he purposed his voyage, he answered, to
Zaragoza, to be at the jousts in harness, that are held
customarily there every year."

> Don Juan told him that there was one thing in that new
> history, which was, that he should be at a running at the ring in
> that city, as short of invention as poor in mottoes, but most poor
> in liveries, and rich in nothing but simplicities.
>
> —For this matter only —quoth Don Quijote— I will not set
> foot in Zaragoza; and therefore the world shall see what a liar this
> modern historiographer is, and people shall perceive I am not the
> Don Quijote he speaks of.
>
> —You shall do very well —quoth Don Jerónimo—; for there
> be other jousts in Barcelona, where Signior Don Quijote may show
> his valour.
>
> —So I mean to do —quoth Don Quijote—. II. 59

The exemplary duration of the story and the movement of historical events come into alignment as they swing around the center of the mythical renown and presence of the hero-knight, for the novelty is that a "living" character carries on about himself in a book and about that book in the everyday lives of its readers.

The second summer, moving through the historical events of the years 1605-1610-1614 was now both continuous and synchronous to the first, for the hidalgo's age remained unchanged perceptively, and both were now circumscribed by the arc of the ideal mythical history of Don Quijote, with its solar festivals and landscape of spring and summer. Cervantes was almost twenty years in coming to this conception of his mock hero. The exemplary course of his fiction would close with a return to sanity and eventually death. But the span of years of its actual composition had been reduced to an element of his mythical delineation.

The time of Don Quijote's three sallies is the last year in the life of Alonso Quijano; its course is the narrative time, the present tense of his story: a mythical year of perpetual spring and recurring summer.

NOTES TO CHAPTER III

1. *El celoso extremeño*: "No ha muchos años que de un lugar de Extremadura salió un hidalgo, nacido de padres nobles, el cual, como un otro Pródigo, por diversas partes de España, Italia y Flandes anduvo gastando, así los años, como la hacienda," *Novelas ejemplares*, ed. S-B [spelling modernized], II, pp. 148-149.

2. All conjecture on this matter, it seems to me, implies a premise as stated by W. J. Entwistle, *Cervantes*, p. 101 (quoted on p. 21 of my text). Luis Astrana Marín takes for granted, without any basis in fact, the existence of a draft or manuscript of an exemplary novel that would have circulated among Cervantes' friends (between 1598 and 1600?), *Vida ejemplar y heroica de Miguel de Cervantes Saavedra* (Madrid: Instituto Editorial Reus, 1948-1958, 7 vols.), V (1953), pp. 248-249 and passim. Geoffrey Stagg provides more reasonable arguments to assume the decisive matter, that at one point (Ch. 9) Cervantes began to expand a story already in draft-form into a mock history of chivalry, "Sobre el plan primitivo del *Quijote*," *Actas del*

Primer Congreso Internacional de Hispanistas (Oxford: Dolphin Book Co., 1964), pp. 463-471. See also Vicente Gaos, "El primitivo plan del Quijote," in *Claves de literatura española*, I (Madrid: Ediciones Guadarrama, 1971), pp. 167-179.

3.   The Duke of Alba had assembled an army out of veteran Spanish forces stationed in Italy; its vanguard arrived in Brussels on August 9, and the Duke's arrival followed; see John Lynch, *Spain under the Hapsburgs* (Oxford: Basil Blackwell), I, p. 280.

4.   Astrana Marín, IV (1952), pp. 454-456.

5.   Cervantes enlisted in Italy, most likely in the summer of 1570, Astrana Marín, II (1949), pp. 253-254; Jaime Fitzmaurice-Kelly, *Miguel de Cervantes Saavedra, reseña documentada de su vida* (Oxford University Press, 1917), p. 43.

6.   Astrana Marín, II, p. 185ff. Fitzmaurice-Kelly, *Cervantes,* pp. 40-41.

7.   *El pastor de Iberia* (Seville, 1591), by Bernardo de la Vega; *Primera parte de las ninphas y pastores de Henares* (Alcalá, 1587), by Bernardo González de Bobadilla; and *Desengaño de celos* (Madrid, 1586), by Bartolomé López de Enciso. These mediocre productions belong to the pastoral genre; few other works published after 1585 are mentioned in the scrutiny. See Entwistle, *Cervantes,* pp. 115-117.

8.   It is generally thought that Cervantes was imprisoned in Seville for about three months, from September to December, 1597 (Fitzmaurice-Kelly, pp. 126-128). Astrana Marín, however, believes that Cervantes was kept in the jail at Seville for a much longer period, until April of 1598, V, p. 241.

9.   Cf. Américo Castro, "Los Prólogos al *Quijote,*" *Hacia Cervantes*, 3rd ed. (Madrid: Taurus, 1967), p. 264.

10.   On the texts (and variants) of the sonnet see Schevill-Bonilla, *Poesías sueltas,* in vol. 6 of *Comedias y Entremeses,* pp. 73-76; also Astrana Marín, V, pp. 321-323. Trans. in: James Y. Gibson, *Journey to Parnassus,* trans. into English tercets with Preface and Illustrative Notes (London: Kegan Paul, Trench & Co., 1883), p. 375.

11.   The first sentence of the story, and indeed the entire first paragraph, is a stylistic combination of traditional formulas and proverbial phrases. "En un lugar de la Mancha" recasts the formula "En un lugar . . ." in the form of a verse, perhaps recalled from an anonymous ballad, see *Flores del Parnaso, Octava Parte,* recopilado por Luys de Medina, Toledo, 1596, ed. Antonio Rodríguez Moñino, *Fuentes del Romancero general de 1600* (Madrid: Real Academia Española, 1957), X, folio 112 verso. ". . . de cuyo nombre no quiero acordarme" repeats an age-old formula of story tellers, and "no quiero" serves as an auxiliary verb. Cf. Don Juan Manuel, *El conde Lucanor,* "En una tierra de que non me acuerdo el nombre había un rey . . . ." Exemplo 51. See María Rosa Lida, "De cuyo nombre no quiero acordarme . . ." *Revista de Filología Hispánica*, 1: 167-171 (1939). This combination produces from the start, and unlike the other (exemplary) stories by Cervantes, an air of *burla* and *donaire.* The style of a mock history of chivalry was derived from an exemplary purpose.

12. See Entwistle, "The Birth of Don Quixote," *Cervantes,* p. 106.

13. Entwistle, *Cervantes,* pp. 104-105. R. Menéndez Pidal, *Un aspecto en la elaboración del "Quijote"* (Madrid, 1924, 2.ª ed. aumentada) pp. 27-29, note. In English, "The Genesis of *Don Quixote,*" in *Cervantes across the Centuries,* ed. Angel Flores and M. J. Benardete ([New York: Dryden Press, 1947]; reprint, with corrections, New York: Gordian Press, 1969), p. 37.

14. It is logical to assume that otherwise Cervantes would have included a mention of Lope de Vega's *Arcadia* (1598, 1599), or his *Angelica's Beauty* (1602), since he mentioned Luis Barahona de Soto's *Angelica's Tears* (1586). See Entwistle, *Cervantes,* pp. 116-117.

15. Geoffrey Stagg has proposed a similar but more elaborate conjecture: "The chapters now numbered 10 and 15 formed originally a *continuum* [later] broken in revision to permit the insertion of Chs. 11-14 into the gap so created," "Revision in *Don Quixote,* Part I," in *Hispanic Studies in Honour of I. González Llubera,* ed. Frank Pierce (Oxford: Dolphin Book Co., 1959), pp. 347-366; p. 351. In Spanish: "Cervantes revisa su novela (*Don Quijote,* I Parte)," *Anales de la Universidad de Chile,* año 124, núm. 140: 5-33 (1966).

16. In some modern editions the heading for Chapter 10 in the first edition is replaced by one inserted in 1780 by the Spanish Academy, e.g., Rodríguez Marín, ed. *DQ* [I. 10], I, p. 291, note. See Pierre L. Ullman, "The Heading of Ch. X in the 1605 *Quijote,*" *Forum for Modern Language Studies,* 7: 41-51 (1971).

17. The most complete information assembled on this matter will be found in an unpublished dissertation by Daniel E. Quilter, "The Image of the *Quijote* in the Seventeenth Century," Univ. of Illinois, Urbana, 1962.

18. *Cervantes y los casticismos españoles* (Madrid-Barcelona: Alfaguara, 1966), pp. 48, 60, 66ff.

19. "Estudio preliminar," vol. I, pp. xxx ff., *Don Quijote,* ed. Celina S. de Cortazar e Isaías Lerner (Buenos Aires: Editorial Universitaria, 1969, 2 vols.).

20. Astrana Marín, V, pp. 418, 436, 451-453.

21. Stagg, "Revision," pp. 355ff. His arguments have omitted all references to the fact that the lives of Grisóstomo and Marcela are entwined variously with life in a village and a populated area. Such a situation is not feasible with the isolated and wild heights of Sierra Morena in Ch. 25.

22. See Castro, "Prólogos," *Hacia Cervantes,* pp. 300-301; Juan Bautista Avalle-Arce, "Grisóstomo y Marcela," in *Deslindes cervantinos* (Madrid: Edhigar, 1961), pp. 97-119. In 1863, in the Biblioteca Colombina in Seville, José María Asensio found a ms. containing a version of the poem (entitled "Canción desesperada") and published it, with the statement that it was undoubtedly the original version, written by Cervantes many years before 1604-05. See Leopoldo Rius, *Bibliografía crítica de las obras de Miguel de Cervantes Saavedra* (3 vols. 1895-1905, reprint 1970), II, p. 177, 199. Text of this version also in

Adolfo de Castro, ed., *Varias obras inéditas de Cervantes* (Madrid, 1874), pp. 177-185. As far as I know, no scholar has rejected Asensio's suppositions. See also: Luis Rosales, *Cervantes y la libertad* (Madrid: Sociedad de Estudios y Publicaciones, 1960), II, pp. 486-510; Rodríguez Marín, ed. *DQ* [I. 14] I, p. 375, note 1; Astrana Marín, V, p. 192, note.

23. The emphatic refusal of Ginés de Pasamonte to set out at once for El Toboso with the other slaves includes: "... digo, a tomar nuestra cadena, y a ponernos en camino del Toboso, es pensar que es ahora de noche, *que aún no son las diez del día,* y es pedir a nosotros eso como pedir peras al olmo," I. 22.

24. *Three* nights if we follow the text of the first ed.; but *four* nights according to the insertion in Cuesta's second ed. explaining the theft of Dapple.

25. Astrana Marín, V, pp. 499, 523 .

26. In I. 37, when the captain and Zoraida arrive at the inn it is evening (*"Ya en esto llegaba la noche"*) and the entire company sat down to supper. In I. 42 Cervantes repeats that nightfall is approaching (*"al cerrar la noche"*), etc.; one of various inconsequences uncovered by Clemencín.

27. Rodríguez Marín, ed. *DQ* [I. 28], II, p. 355, note; Astrana Marín, V, pp. 492-495.

28. The figure of Zoraida is based on the same legend that Cervantes dramatized (at a later date, probably) in the play *Los baños de Argel.* The legend and its historical basis have been outlined by Jaime Oliver Asín in an important study, *La hija de Agi Morato en la obra de Cervantes* (Madrid: Imprenta de S. Aguirre, 1948, 101p; published also in *Boletín de la Real Academia Española,* 27: 245-339 (1947-48). Oliver Asín concludes, but does not demonstrate (sec. 36), that the play is the earlier of the two versions of the legend, and this entails a major miscalculation in his comparison of them. In a study just published, Franco Meregalli argues for a late date of the *Baños,* between 1607-1608 and 1615, "De *Los tratos de Argel* a *Los baños de Argel,*" *Homenaje a* [Joaquín] *Casalduero* (Madrid: Gredos, 1972), pp. 395-409; see p. 402. Meregalli, on the other hand, is apparently unaware of Oliver Asín's study (reviewed in *Anales cervantinos,* I: 369-371 (1951), and hence fails to make a definitive point about the relations between Cervantes' story, *Los baños* and *Los tratos* and Lope de Vega's *Los cautivos de Argel.*

According to the information made available by Oliver Asín, one may assume that in the years of Cervantes' captivity in Algiers (1575-1580) there arose among the Spanish Christians held captive in that city the legend of a daughter of a wealthy moor who had fallen in love with one of their number and wished to become a Christian. Most likely a successful escape to Spain was part of this legend. For reasons that can only be conjectured, this legend became associated with the daughter of a wealthy Algerian, Ḥāǧǧī Murād, or 'Agi Morato.' Her name was Zahara, the name Cervantes gives to his heroine in the play. What we know of the historical Zahara has only the most tenuous connection with the version of the legend we find in the story or the play. The historical Zahara was married twice, to men of power and wealth in Algiers. Her first husband was 'Abd al-Malik, whom she married probably in 1574, and to whom she bore a son, and who ruled as sultan of Morocco (Marruecos) in 1576 and was killed in 1578 in the battle against the Portuguese at Alcazarquivir. A few years later, most likely in 1580, Zahara married Hasan Bāšā, or 'Hasán Bajá,' who, of course, was Cervantes' master and owner in Algiers (after 1577). Agi Morato was a renegade, a fact most likely known to Cervantes. Zahara's maternal grandmother was a Mallorcan taken captive in 1529. The Christian background of her grandparents was probably one of the reasons why the legend of a daughter of a wealthy moor who escaped to Spain with a Christian slave she helped liberate became associated with the Zahara of history who, after 1580, lived in Constantinople as the wife of a powerful Moslem. In the story Agi Morato is never disclosed as a renegade (nor is Zoraida conceived as the "conversa" that she will be). The picture of Zoraida in the story is probably drawn according to Cervantes' recollections of what the historical Zahara was like as a young girl in 1575-76, whereas the captain suggests a character pictured in the years 1589-90. Which is to say that whatever historical figures or chronology we may find reflected in the story are subordinated to the idealized account of the love between a nineteen-year-old girl and a soldier turned forty.

29. By 1604 the Spanish *comedia* and theaters had reached the significant first stage of their maturity, but this is the latest stage to which Cervantes' remarks could apply. Cf. N. D. Shergold, *A History of the Spanish Stage* (Oxford: Clarendon Press, 1967), p. 209.

30. On the analogies between Lope de Vega's *comedias* and Cervantes' *novelas* see Marcos A. Morínigo, "El teatro como sustituto de la novela en el Siglo de Oro," *Revista de la Universidad de Buenos Aires*, 5.ª época, año 2, núm. 2: 41-61 (1957), the item cited in note 19 above, and my article, "Don Quijote, *nuevo* caballero," *Estudios ... ofrecidos a Marcos A. Morínigo* (Madrid: Insula, 1971), pp. 91-102.

31. The prophecy is, of course, a conception belonging to 'magical' and 'mythical' time, as believed in by Don Quijote and Sancho. Their belief can be reduced to a psychological explanation and a 'psychological' or 'personal time.'

32. It is questionable whether the last two declarations of a 'chronological' nature mean very much in terms of narrative duration (see Clemencín's notes). The fight with the goatherd ends when the sound of a trumpet breaks from a hilltop. A group of penitents appears, and we are told that this is a procession on its way to a holy shrine, to plead for rain in a dry year. Clemencín noted that if (as Ríos claimed) this is a day in September, it is the time of the harvest when any rain is unwelcomed, in fact the very worst time of the year to pray for rain. A dry spell is damaging to crops in the season of their growth, and such a rogation for rain is much more feasible within a prolonged dry spell in spring or early summer. It is not far-fetched to suppose that Cervantes could have been thinking already of a time for a third sally, that is, of a re-beginning, and hence of a recurrent spring or

summer. The other declaration is Sancho's outburst over his master's prostrate body. So generous was his master, he says, that for "only eight months service" he had given him "the best island in the sea." This hyperbole is in line with all other declarations about the island. It is no more a precise total of his service than a clear statement of whether his master gave and delivered, or simply promised the island to him.

33. The last portions of the book to be written were the Prologue and Dedication. In fact the Prologue and not the valedictory poems are the genuine epilogue, see Castro, "Prólogos," p. 262. In the final poems, as in the preliminary, there are enough inconsistencies or contradictions to the story to suspect that some (and perhaps all) were not written by Cervantes, but by friends of his. See Marcel Bataillon, "Urganda entre *Don Quijote* y *La Pícara Justina*," *Varia lección de clásicos españoles* (Madrid: Gredos, 1964), pp. 296-299. One should remark that it is unlike Cervantes even to suggest that "Argamasilla" was Don Quijote's village or *patria*.

34. On the reception of *Don Quijote* in the seventeenth century and in particular the years 1605-1610, see Miguel Herrero García, *Estimaciones literarias del siglo XVII* (Madrid: Editorial Voluntad, 1930,) pp. 353-420; Alberto Navarro, *El "Quijote" español del siglo XVII* (Madrid: Ediciones Rialp, 1964), pp. 255-321; Quilter, op. cit., Ch. 2; Astrana Marín, VI (1956), pp. 195-197.

35. See the detailed account by José Terrero, "Las rutas de las tres salidas de don Quijote de la Mancha," *Anales cervantinos*, 8: 1-49 (1959-60), and "Itinerario del *Quijote* de Avellaneda y su influencia en el cervantino," *Anales cervantinos*, 2: 159-191 (1952).

36. My conjecture breaks down to this — in phase one: the composition of all materials, drafts, revisions, from 1607 or 1610 to the appearance of *Novelas ejemplares* and its Prologue; in phase two: from this point in 1613 to the date Cervantes learned of Avellaneda's imitation (September or October, 1614); in phase three: to the date of the book's completion.

37. See M. A. Buchanan (who favors the dates 1611-1613), "The works of Cervantes and their dates of composition," *Transactions of the Royal Society of Canada*, 3rd series, sec. 2, vol. 32: 23-39 (1938); p. 34. Astrana Marín favors the year 1607, VI, pp. 233-235. Almost all speculation on this point is based on the number of editions of the First Part one may presume are mentioned in II. 3, and the number of copies in circulation. The situation would seem to correspond to any of the years 1608 to 1611, and later. By 1608 (the date of Cuestas' third ed.) it would be known in Madrid that the First Part had been printed in the Low Countries (Brussels, *not* Antwerp, 1607, and then in 1611), and the number of editions (8) then known would roughly account for "twelve thousand copies," see ed. RM, IV, note p. 82. Astrana Marín, loc. cit., also supposes that as Cervantes completed successive chapters from 1607 to 1614, he turned them over to Francisco de Robles, who paid him for them in installments, and that this explains why Cervantes was unable to correct obvious

oversights, errors, and inconsistencies. This supposition, whatever its merits, would make untenable any idea that Cervantes was able to carry out revisions in 1614 on his earlier chapters as conjectured by Riquer, see note 41 below.

38.   We cannot be certain that Cervantes had any knowledge of the translations by Shelton (1612) and Oudin (1614). Carrasco's statements are more in the way of intuition and prophecy, and thus all the more remarkable.

39.   The number of editions of the First Part that Cervantes could have known about in 1607-08 was eight, and in 1612-13 ten. The statement is apparently a quixotic exaggeration. However, see Buchanan, op. cit., p. 35.

40.   It is now included in the collection of Clásicos Castellanos (Madrid: Espasa-Calpe, 1972, 3 vols.), edited and with an introduction by Martín de Riquer. See his bibliography, vol. I.

41.   My remarks rest on the general premise that has been the starting point for all discussions of Cervantes' knowledge of Avellaneda's book, or the latter's knowledge of the authentic Second Part, while Cervantes was in the process of writing it. The premise may be stated thus: because Cervantes incorporated into the composition and plot of his own Second Part a discussion of Avellaneda's book, thereby absorbing it into the fabric of his own story, that discussion in Ch. 59 corresponds to the point in the process of composition when Cervantes first informed himself of the contents of the false sequel. Therefore, all knowledge of the contents of Avellaneda's book, and its effect and influence on the work in progress, begins at this point in time (my assumption is that this took place in September or October of 1614). In 1920 Menéndez Pidal found this premise untenable and spoke of an influence of Avellaneda on Cervantes previous to the publication of the apocryphal version, *Un aspecto*, pp. 64-65 (see note 13 above). In other words, Cervantes had worked on his Second Part with some knowledge of the contents of Avellaneda's book before it appeared in print, and hence Avellaneda's version had been influential in the body of Cervantes' story. Thirty years later Stephen Gilman reviewed the entire question and studied in particular those similarities that would lead one to suspect that Cervantes knew some details of Avellaneda's version before it was published, that is, similarities in his story previous to Ch. 59, *Cervantes y Avellaneda, estudio de una imitación* (Colegio de México, 1951), pp. 167-176. He concluded that it was more logical to assume that the similarities between Cervantes' story previous to Ch. 59 and Avellaneda's were the result of plagiarism on the part of Avellaneda. The imitator had had some knowledge of the story Cervantes was working on, in 1613 and 1614, and copied him. But just recently Martín de Riquer has added a new seriousness to the whole question, Introd., Clás. Cast., pp. xxxv-xxxix. He holds that the similarities in the story previous to Ch. 59 (e.g., Master Peter's puppet show, Sancho's letter to Teresa, etc.) are a result of Cervantes imitating (and thus outstripping) Avellaneda, but he prefers to believe that they were introduced as revisions (some of them extensive) on

portions of the story Cervantes had written before he saw a printed copy of Avellaneda's book. In my opinion the greater part of the evidence (still) supports Gilman's position, but the question is far from solved.

IV

THE SUMMER OF MYTH

MYTHICAL TIME: SOLAR CYCLES AND SUN GODS

T H E knight Don Quijote who greets the sunrise over the
fields of La Mancha is as much a descendant of the gods of
solar mythology as the paragons of chivalry he emulates. His
world, like theirs, traces the word-picture of solar myths, and,
like theirs, his trajectory in time and space describes the
processional cycles of the sun. The summer of myth is
the illusion sustained by Don Quijote as the time and season
of his career as a knight, an illusion in turn sustained as an
exemplary fiction by the parodic styles of Cervantes the
novelist. As such the mock hero, a fusion of psychosis and
myth, has the complex symptoms of a major clinical and literary case.

The heroes of chivalric romance are literary creatures the
storied outlines of whose quests and trials are based on
the course of the sun through the seasons as depicted in
countless mythical tales. The remote origins of Arthurian
heroes like Yvain, Lancelot, and Gawain can be traced back
through folk tales and legends to primitive Celtic myths.
Lancelot, according to the best authority, [1] descends from
the great sun and storm gods of the Gauls and Irish. Gawain's
antecedents in mythology are solar heroes eternally young
whose strength would wax with the mounting sun and wane
as it declined. [2] As mythical conceptions their stories tell of
struggles and feats that trace the course of the sun across
the heavens in its daily and seasonal movement. The struggle
of the sun gods against darkness, the conflict of solar heroes
against the powers of evil and death, are mythical conceptions
transmuted into stories of knights drawn in battle against evil

forces, who wane or withdraw as winter approaches, or come forth to triumph at midsummer.

The origins of the temporal pattern that concerns us can be traced to elements of solar and seasonal myths worked into the fabric of chivalric stories and histories in the twelfth century. In this decisive phase of its development chivalric romance transmuted a wonderful but dispersed lore of folk traditions rooted in primitive Celtic rituals and myths (tales, magic, festivals) into a picture of a legendary past presumed to be the time of King Arthur and his court (the fifth century), but a picture of such relative social stability that the king and his knights moved or wandered almost at will from castle or court to forest or wilderness, across vast and distant kingdoms, in a pattern of wars, processions and festivals unfolding in the cyclical course of the seasons. The story patterns evolved by Chrétien de Troyes and other poets and their followers were embroidered on the temporal outlines of Christian ceremony and ritual which in turn traced the archaic lines of solar and seasonal mythologies. Thus the course of adventures and trials of heroes like Gawain and Lancelot, with its cyclical duration sustained from one year to the next, was an elaboration upon seasonal or ritual myths, where the contending forces of winter and summer sought to subject or liberate an earthmaiden or vegetation goddess. [3] And if solar heroes and moon or vegetation goddesses are the principals in ritual stories of fertility, birth, death, and growth, the water spirits, fays and fairies are only slightly lesser embodiments of natural forms and forces in the struggle between light and darkness, life and death. But having passed from mythologies and folk tales and traditions into the Arthurian legends and become creatures of romance, they are here, with King Arthur, the exalted figures of courtly and chivalric pageantry, embodiments of passions and powers, of noble and good forces, — of bravery, manly conscience and courtesy, like Lancelot and Gawain; — of feminine beauty and grace and near-inviolate chastity, like Guenievre, or the assorted ladies or dames of the court, or enchantresses like

Morgan the Fay, or Urganda la desconocida; — or the discreet and clever damsels, whose freedom and autonomy, like their chastity, is as much an article of belief to Don Quijote as incredible to Cervantes (*DQ*. I. 9).

The temporal pattern of chivalric romance corresponds thus to the exalted and legendary quality of its principal figures. The course of their movements is solar pageantry and therefore the season of their depictment on the solar cycle is the arc running from Easter to midsummer. Here then is the nuclear relation between the time pattern derived from early myths and the story patterns of romance that depicts knightly adventures in the cyclical course of seasons and festivals, with an inveterate preference for spring and summer. The two characteristics of time elements in medieval Arthurian romance is the pattern that fits the succession of tests and trials of strength, or of love and loyalty, within the course of solar feastdays on the Christian liturgical calendar and the concentration of events in the cycle of spring festivals, running from the vernal equinox to midsummer: Easter, Whitsuntide, Ascension Day, Saint John's Day. The narrative can either move forward with the solar cycle from one spring to the next, or else appear to be stationary in time, in a land of perpetual spring-like summer. [4] The former conception allows for movement, the latter appears to suspend the story in a mythical time and place. It is remarkable that precisely in the finest productions of medieval romance do we find temporal patterns traceable to mythical concepts clearly evidenced.

The fourteenth-century Middle English romance *Sir Gawain and the Green Knight* tells a story of a challenge by a mysterious knight (*Green* is a transposition of *grey*, the traditional color in a Welsh tradition for horse and outfit of 'Winter' [5]) and a lone quest by the young hero, beginning at Christmas and New Year's Day and moving through (vss. 491-536) the interval of one year to its climax at dawn on the next New Year. Gawain and the Green Knight are analogues of mythical personifications of Summer and Winter, and their annual conflict enacted in the ritual slaying of a solar divinity and his replacement by another at the time of the winter solstice. The wife of the Green Knight, who on orders from her husband tempts the young hero, is a transposition of the ladies of inviolate chastity involved in the mythical stories of combats of summer kings and their opponents. [6] Gawain's chaste conduct is thus in line with the precedents for Don Quijote's concern for his chastity. Both, it seems, are transmutations of the motif of an inviolate chastity of feminine figures. The Green Knight is an embodiment of 'Lord of Winter' and his storms and of the Wild Huntsman who appeared with his baying hounds (the wind blasts), particularly between Christmas and Twelfth Night, of various Welsh folk traditions, tales, and festivals. Gawain, according to the same, is 'Lord of Summer' ('Summer White'). It is a Welsh tradition that gives us a story pattern of the annual beheading of a solar figure by his replacement within a temporal pattern that begins and ends the story on New Year's. [7] The more usual Celtic tradition favored a pattern that set the annual conflict on the date of the great May festival (May 1) that marked the beginning of summer. Likewise, as noted in the scheme followed by the unknown poet of *Gawain* (vs. 536), the beginning of winter was set at All Hallows (November 1).

Variations of the same cyclical pattern are found in Chrétien de Troyes' *Yvain, le Chevalier au Lion* (ca. 1175). The action in the first portion of his poem takes place in the interval of two weeks between the spring feast of Pentecost (Whitsuntide) and the feast of The Nativity of Saint John the Baptist. King Arthur holds a court at Carduel on the feast day of Pentecost. Here Yvain hears the story of the perilous spring in the forest of Broceliande and sets out in secret to look for it immediately, for the king also intends to go there with his court and arrive by the Vigil of the Feast of Saint John. [8] Yvain finds the marvelous fountain, pours water over the stone, causes the storm, and defeats the storm-knight of the spring. He marries Laudine, the wife

of the slain knight, and when Arthur arrives he welcomes the
king at midsummer as the defender of the spring and its
marvels. After a week of festivities, the king prepares to
depart. Yvain wishes to accompany him, and requests his
wife's permission. She consents on the condition that he will
return within a year's time, by the eighth day after the Feast
of Saint John. Yvain devotes himself so completely to travels
and feats of arms in the year's interval that he forgets his
promise and fails to return by the date set by his wife. When
in mid-August (feast of the Assumption) he is at Chester,
where the King is holding a court, she sends word to him
that she has withdrawn her affection and has banished him
forever from her presence. Struck with remorse, Yvain falls
into a state of violent madness; he tears his flesh and strips
off his clothing. In his madness he reverts to a wild state;
wandering unclothed, he hunts beasts and eats their raw flesh
like a savage. He lives in a forest, a wilderness, until he meets
a hermit who makes possible his return to civilized life. In
Yvain's madness we have the genesis of the topic — the knight
who goes (temporarily) mad and reverts to a 'wild state'
because he has offended his lady — that will reach the
author(s) of *Amadís de Gaula* by way of the legends of
Lancelot, Tristan, and eventually Cervantes. [9] The episode
of Sierra Morena, we know, takes place in August. Is it only
coincidence that Chrétien and Cervantes — centuries apart —
set the date of their hero's madness in August? Yvain is
eventually reconciled to his wife, after he kills the serpent
and frees the lion. His rescue of the lion is also the precedent
for associating this noble beast to the person of a knight that
is the basis for Cervantes' episode of the lions in Part Two. [10]
Both Yvain's madness and his association with the lion are
situations created by Chrétien out of motifs and traditions
reaching back into early Christian and pagan legends, tales
and mythology.

Chrétien is also, of course, the creator of the knight who
— after the four centuries that saw his legend adapted to
popular ballads in Castile — is rejuvenated and recreated

in Don Quijote's illusion of himself: Lancelot. The magic of
the name *Lanzarote* is always present to Cervantes and his
hidalgo, but apparently they knew little more about his legend than is told in the famous ballad. [11] Neither seems
to be aware that they tread on the precincts of the greatest
story of adulterous love in all of literature. For that is what
the Arthurian legend and the courtly tradition made subsequently of Chrétien's narrative. [12] As romance in the courtly
sense the love between Guenievre and Lancelot is the story
of a passion awakened in an older, voluptuous woman and
queen by an adoring boy, who is also the finest knight in
bravery, skill and service. As told by Chrétien, it is an abduction story embroidered over the outlines of a seasonal myth.
Guenievre is abducted by Meleagant and taken to a seemingly
inaccessible kingdom. Lancelot is her rescuer, having replaced
the King and husband in this role. [13] The combats for her
possession are twice broken off, and then a year's interval
elapses before the final battle. The outlines of a seasonal
myth involving the abduction of an earth-maiden or vegetation
goddess by forces embodied in a divine or royal figure (King
of Winter), her imprisonment in the Other World during
winter, and her liberation by a summer deity (King of Summer), are discernible in the pattern that sets the beginning
of the story and the Queen's abduction on the May festival of
Ascension Day, and brings it to a close on the same date,
in a wood where the herbage is fresh at all seasons, and
reminiscent of the land of perpetual, springlike summer. [14]
Moreover, that the Queen was not ravished by her abductor,
that her chastity and honor have emerged unscathed, is a
derivation from the inviolate chastity of the earth-bride or
abducted maiden of Celtic mythology.

Medieval romance was then invested with a temporal scale
the equal of its resplendent personages. This scale not only
served to depict the cosmic pageant of their quests, trials,
and passionate relationships, it was, so to speak, the space-
time configuration of their existence, for like them it was
evolved from mythological concepts. So long as their authors

conceived these resplendent figures as creatures of romance would such a scale serve to enlarge or enhance their depiction. In romance, accordingly, the structure of fictional duration is cyclical, and time and space a progression upon the landscape of the seasonal course of solar light and motion. The narrative is of course sequential and episodic, and various adventures might be aligned, interlaced, or grouped around the principal quest. But the climax of trials or quests comes about on the great solar festivals because their duration and progression revolve with the great cycle of solar movement. Hence, narrative time, and with it the plot and its motivations, follows the course of the seasons, and is cyclical in movement, as each of the important festivals becomes a setting for tournaments, reunions, and processions. Perhaps the first instance of such ceremonies is the great plenary court at Whitsuntide that King Arthur holds in a certain passage of Geoffrey of Monmouth's *Historia Regum Britanniae* (IX, 12). In the French romances it is usual for King Arthur to hold court five times a year on the great Christian festivals: Easter, Ascension, Whitsuntide, All Saints and Christmas. But the full cycle of feastdays would be, beginning with the spring equinox: Easter, Whitsun, Ascension Day, Saint John's Day, the Assumption (mid-August), All-Hallows, Christmas and (in England) New Year's.

Yet the materials of romance were also assumed to be at least vaguely historical by its authors, and hence they also conceived the events of their stories within a chronology patterned after the medieval chronicle. The point need not be pressed. It is sufficient to say that story *(conte)* and history *(histoire, estoire,* etc.) were never clearly defined nor differentiated among medieval storytellers. The large scale of the narrative in the extensive prose cycles, whose duration was conceived as lasting for many years, was an outgrowth of the same tendencies that saw the compilations of vast histories in the vernacular. The writers of romance adapted the outline form of a chronicle as a framework because it was as much a part of the tradition that had preserved the story as the story

was. When Chrétien uses the formula "Et dit li contes, se
me sanble...." (*Yvain*, vs. 2685) he is making an explicit
reference to an earlier and supposedly authoritative version.
And so in the Vulgate Lancelot: "Or dist li contes que quant
lancelot se fu partis de la chambre ou il ot este souspris...." [15]
In *Amadís de Gaula* a further claim is made for an authoritative *order* in the story: "Pero, porque a la orden de la
hystoria assí cumple, antes vos contaremos algo de lo que en
aquel medio de tiempo acaesció." (Bk. 2, Ch. 48, p. 398) The
extensive prose romances like the *Lancelot* and the *Amadís*
are biographical, that is they tell the complete story of the
chivalric hero much in the way of an historical biography
or chronicle, and hence the chronological order of the narrative assumes a pseudo-historical framework. [16] In the sixteenth-century Spanish romances these formulaic devices were
somewhat crudely used to strengthen claims of historical
authenticity, and it is to these bogus claims that Cervantes
pointed his parody. The medieval romancers may not have
felt obliged to make such claims, yet it is evident that in the
prose versions dating from the thirteenth century an historical
concept served to support the time pattern of their stories,
and most notably where the mythological elements slackened
them.

To recapitulate: the heroes of chivalric romance are literary creatures who undergo trials and undertake adventures
in a legendary space and time derived from mythical and
ritual lore, folktales, and magic, but depicted and intended
to be taken as historical. The temporal pattern of their stories,
with their quests, annual combats, rituals and ceremonies,
is in many respects a solar mythology overlaid with pagan
and Christian seasonal festivals in observance of solar motion.
A chronicle concept in the longer prose versions binds together as one both duration and succession, and is, one may
suppose, an approach to realism, but the actual depiction of
events is a span of time revolving around the seasonal festivals
of spring and summer. In the due passage of time journeys
are undergone and adventures undertaken, but the time of

the narrative is the constant of a summery season, the romantic time of a depiction of fabulous and passionate creatures. Behind the movement of solar and natural time, behind the pageantry unfolding in the course of human lives and history, is the season of romance, a space-time configuration of narrative duration within a cyclical movement. This temporal pattern points to an ideal land of a perpetual spring-like summer suspended in time and related to the enchanted or otherworld regions, like the isle of Avalon or the *aestiva regio* ("Summer Land") of Arthurian romance, or the Classical and Celtic Elysium, evoked in myths of paradise and the golden age.

THE GOLDEN AGE

—Sancho amigo, has de saber que yo nací, por querer del cielo, en esta nuestra edad de hierro, para resucitar en ella la de oro, o la dorada, como suele llamarse.

—*Friend Sancho, I would have thee know that I was born, by the disposition of heaven, in this our age of iron, to resuscitate in it that of gold, or the golden world, as it is called.*

The scene is night in the dark wood; there falls a horrible, fearful sound of blows and cascading water ahead:

Yo soy aquel para quien están guardados los peligros, las grandes hazañas, los valerosos hechos. I. 20

I am he for whom are reserved all dangerous, great, and valorous feats. I. 20

In order to live his illusion as a complete experience that is both a triumph of the senses and of will-power, Don Quijote projects himself into the mythical time of a chivalric quest. In that, *sensu stricto*, narrative time there is no essential difference between him and the knights he surpasses. The difference is only one of degree. He surpasses them. For him the entire span of his adventures takes place on the plane of mythical possibilities and fulfilment. The dynamic of his illusion is to sustain the image of himself in a mythical role and time. I say dynamic because to sustain that image he must keep it aglow in expectation of his fame. Inwardly his test is to undergo the ordeal of the elect among knights, to feel the moral challenge of one whose strength, valor, and nobility are expended in a struggle against supernatural antagonists, and in travail and suffering on behalf of the weak and defenseless. The sign of his elect being is the fame that confirms it by progressively magnifying itself. His quest is thus to achieve the renown of literary heroes and to become the most famous of knights, as the fulfillment of an inner need and impulse. In this the subjective sense of his adventures neither the season nor the landscape have any great importance. They are the adjuncts of that span of prophetic time that stretches from the fabled narratives of his models into the felicitous future of his fame. Or to put it another way, the mythical picture of himself is timeless, because knighthood is not a dead past but a present challenge fraught with dynamic possibilities, and because the present time and his identity as an hidalgo have been effaced.

Yet Cervantes provided the outward conformity of his outings to the seasonal setting of romance by depicting them in summer. The mythical conception of himself held by the mock hero is correspondingly re-created in the pattern of duration and seasonal landcape. In Part One it is sequential and exemplary. Two outings in the course of a few weeks in July and August are a satirical contrast to the magnificent scale of adventures in the romances of chivalry. But in Part Two Cervantes was induced to devise a "cyclical" and "mythical" pattern of duration and movement along the arc of spring festivals that confirmed the renown of Don Quijote in his book and in the historical world. Thus, if the summer of Part One may be called the summer of the exemplary time of his narrative, the spring and summer of Part Two may be called the summer of myth, for here the similitude of Don Quijote's fame to the mythical renown of literary knights is a structural factor in the narrative, that is to say, the growth of his fame is part of the process of becoming.

That the narrative of Part Two should move forward from April to July and August, and then (Chs. 59-61) revert to midsummer upon Don Quijote's arrival at Barcelona, is a consequence of the merger of exemplary and romantic time. As the climax of the narrative the scene of arrival had perforce to consummate the mythical year of a perpetual spring-like summer that was concomitant in the mythical plan of Part Two. Yet narrative movement in the first summer, as we shall now see, is also pressed forward by mythical elements at work in an exemplary story.

In the design of Part One Don Quijote's fame is but a tissue of his literary psychosis. His two outings take place in a few weeks of a summer period because the parody and satire of chivalric adventure are to have a realistic basis. But from the start the hidalgo has performed all of his actions in a time of his illusions. Accordingly, one of the satirical meanings of his lyrical outbursts on greeting the dawn on that first morning is that, imagining himself to be a young man with the passion and prowess of Amadís, he feels youthful, rejuvenated. He evokes a spring dawn because he feels youthful, and because he is in love with a girl-princess, Dulcinea. The illusion of his knighthood is the image of his rejuvenescence, and hence the time and season of his adventure is the spring-like summer of romance and poetic myth. It is this romantic season that holds the promise of his mythical fame.

This seems to me a necessary connective between his evocation of a mythical sunrise and his evocation of the golden age in Chapter Eleven. Now these two conceptions are essentially timeless, that is, dynamic *and* conceptual, as instigators, as vitalizers. However erratic his hold on myth, or reality, it serves to impel him precisely as it disengages him from the time and space of his hidalgo's existence. It motivates him, so to speak, in the absence of real motives arising from real situations, to the gratuitous act. An act conceived or motivated in relation to a timeless concept is nonetheless performed in a present time. How, then, does

Don Quijote relate his timeless, that is, mythical, enterprise
to the sensible facts of the environment he wishes to mold to
his ideal?

His evocation of the idyllic golden age is not just a mo-
tionless picture of a static condition, even less the rhetorical
exercise most Cervantean critics see. A thousand readers of
Cervantes have intuited that here Don Quijote infused the
myth of the golden age with a prophetic role (and therefore
with another myth) for his chivalry (as an instance of Renaissance utopianism), and thereby displaced its traditional as-
sociations with the pastoral, but how many critics have
thought it worth pointing out? [17]

His discourse has what we might call a "rhetorical"
movement that prefigures the narrative and temporal movement of major adventures in Part Two, the cave of Montesinos, Clavileño, and even the puppet play. These episodes
revolve around the idea of a quest reserved prophetically and
exclusively for Don Quijote. Here in the discourse there is
a similar line of disclosures toward a prophetic statement,
and encased in a classical temporal concept. Of interest is
the fact that in Chapter Nine the author had interjected these
phrases as he prepared to continue his *history:* "nuestro famoso español don Quijote de la Mancha, luz y espejo de la
caballería manchega, y el primero que en nuestra edad y en
estos tan calamitosos tiempos se puso al trabajo y ejercicio de
las andantes armas"; "our famous Spaniard, Don Quijote of
the Mancha, the light and mirror of all Manchical chivalry,
being the first who, in this our age and time, so full of
calamities, did undergo the travels and exercise of arms-
errant." *In these calamitous times* ... Here then is the inter-
diction on the present time that predicates a redemptive role
for him. The acorns held in his hand, following the repast
shared with the goatherds, provokes the comparison between
the arcadian past and the vices of the detestable present. And
it is precisely on the subject of feminine chastity that the
present times are inveighed against. "Maidens and honesty
wandered then, I say, where they listed, alone, signiorising,

secure, that no stranger, liberty, or lascivious intent could prejudice it, and only their own native desire or will any way endamage it. But now, in these our detestable times, no damsel is safe, although she be hid and shut up in another new labyrinth, like that of Crete...." (the damsels of a Celtic tradition have moved onto a Greco-Roman landscape, or, what amounts to the same, a pastoral landscape is replaced by a chivalric one). The movement of his oratory has swung from the bucolic *(zagalejas)* to the chivalric *(doncellas)*, and leads eventually to himself: "for whose protection and security was last instituted, by success of times, the order of knighthood, ... Of this order am I, friends goatherds...."

What is remarkable here is not so much that Don Quijote has redirected toward himself a vision of the golden age, with the nostalgia or misgivings it excited in certain poetic spirits of the sixteenth century, but that he evokes it knowledgeably from the vantage ground of, ... so to speak, the distillation of myth that are anthropology and history. The golden age is after all a part of the classical concept about a progressive decay of mankind, through the silver, bronze and iron ages. If the golden age, like the Garden of Eden, is outside of time, the iron age is historical time, evolutionary, progressive. The present age of iron malice and necessity is the consequence of an irreversible process. Of course this 'historical process' of his psychosis leads to knighthood. It is not *the* historical process, according to Hegel, that has antiquated it. In the quixotic mentality the present iron age is devoid of a sustaining myth; the golden age seems lost irretrievably; the life-giving myth is the one that will gather up the past and project it into the future, prophetic, utopian. [18]

Thus his obsession and illusion feed on two 'modern' myths, one of the golden age and subsequent moral decay of man, and the other of an advance toward a utopian or messianic future. In sixteenth-century Spain these were not yet 'ideas'; they were commonplace notions of humanistic concern, unattached to any systematic explanation, whether Christian theology, modern or classical philosophy, historical or scientific thought. Cervantes endowed his character with a knowledge of one and an intuition of the other, nearly compelling him to improvise his new chivalry as their resolution. To revive the golden age would mean not just to end and reform these "detestable times," but to bring time to the consummation of a utopian order.

However we might explain Don Quijote's view of history, we shall find it shaped to fit his conception of a prophetic role for chivalry, encarnate in himself. Thus the present time of his adventures is shown a constant instigation of incentive and rewards, expectations and incitements, as he lives inwardly the challenge to heroic deportment, within the extremes of depression and melancholy and choleric outbursts. In the second discourse a similar movement in his rhetorical skill brings him to the subject of firearms: "Those blessed ages were fortunate which wanted the dreadful fury of the devilish and murdering pieces of ordnance.... I am about to say that it grieves me to have ever undertaken the exercise of a knight-errant in this our detestable age...." I. 38.

MYTHICAL TIME: BELTENEBROS

The reader who reacts to Cervantes' exemplary effect perceives that Don Quijote lives his experiences as fully as sensation and imagination allow. He lives them outwardly as an eventful saturation of the senses and an exalted image of himself, inwardly as a consummation of sensory and imaginative needs. What he traces in his mind as a chivalrous adventure is a situation conventionalized in literary traditions, but that now opens up before him as the propitious occasion for asserting his role as a knight. The image of his knighthood, constantly excited by his senses, is sustained by the immediacy with which he expects events to fulfill his expectations. Thus, in the here and now of the fullness of his senses, he lives in the mythical time and space that unfold according to his illusions and toward their imminent realization. We might say that he recreates the mythical content of chivalric adventure, but for him their time is not a past or archaic time but the present one of his desires, exertions, and imaginative needs. Or, in other words, that there is no temporal difference between his actions and those depicted in chivalric and romantic adventures, with their effusions of magic and enchantments, their design of cause and effect, motivations and outcome. It follows that this 'mythical time' suspended in anticipation will bring to pass the effectuality of Don Quijote in the world of sense experience and cause and effect, where the outcome is as precise as anticipation has drawn it. Here and now in this 'mythical time' he slays giants and the feminine figure who approaches his bed is the perfumed lady and princess overcome by his attraction. In this time the magical balsam of Fierabrás works routinely to put back together the mangled body of the hero, the battle of arrayed pagan and Christian armies is decided by the intervention of a knight of incredible prowess, and the wearer of Mambrino's glittering helmet is hailed as invincible. The exemplary effect tells us he is as comically ineffectual in a fictional world as he believes himself to be heroical in the real.

In the unfolding of Cervantes' exemplary design the Sierra Morena episode follows the incident with the galley slaves and is a consequence of his mock hero's deepening mood. The choleric side of his temperament has been played out in the course of adventures from the attack on the windmills to the engagement with the galley slaves, with a violent outburst at its close. His *humor* has now lapsed into a period of melancholy and depression, and Cervantes prepares a parody of the most sentimental of the adventures of knighthood. Cardenio's poems and letters suggested to Don Quijote the very situation that his psycho-physiological condition has prepared for him, the role of the spurned and distraught lover. The hidalgo's narrative autonomy has perforce to be the means for this exemplary parody. His imitation of the grieving, penitent knight is the most sensitive and feeling of his imitative actions, and because it is a conscious and introspective reaching out for a mythical role the most gratuitous. In Chapter 15 Cervantes had already made a reference to Montalvo's episode of the kind his parody could not avoid:

> there hath been a knight that hath dwelt on a rock, exposed to the sun and the shadow, and other annoyances of heaven, for the space of two years, without his lady's knowledge. And Amadís was one of that kind, when, calling himself Beltenebrós, he dwe't in the Poor Rock, nor do I know punctually eight years or eight months, for I do not remember the history well; let it suffice that there he dwelt doing of penance, for some disgust which I know not, that his lady, Oriana, did him. I. 15

Don Quijote cannot recall a more or less definite duration because none is ever specified or even suggested. In *Amadís de Gaula* the tone and essence of Beltenebrós' penance on the Peña Pobre is romantic sentiment. [19] As recounted by Montalvo, it is a notable composite of literary elements; some with a long and obscure history reaching back into legends of penitent saints of early Christianity are merged with others from folklore and myth, and among them is 'the wild man.' [20] Montalvo's episode is the most complete treatment in Spanish of the chivalric topic of the knight who goes mad (or nearly so) for reasons of love and as a consequence of his derangement reverts to a wild state. But while implicit in the role of the social outcast that he assumes on receiving Oriana's vehement letter, Amadís' wild state is not carried to any but a sentimental excess. Beltenebrós is throughout a chivalric hero of sentiment, or even the sentimental hero. He is not driven to commit violent or destructive acts. His love madness is not primarily a loss of reason but a derangement of the senses in the form of an overwhelming anguish that affects the mind. An anguish so acute that it brings on a psychotic depression and despair. The picture is a wasted knight, sobbing, sighing, and weeping constantly:

> Beltenebrós was sitting at this time by the fountain under the trees, ... where he passed the night, and his health was now so spent that he did not expect to live fifteen days, and what with much weeping, and his extreme thinness, his face was very wasted and dark, much more so than if he were suffering from a grave illness.... [21]

So complete is the havoc to his feelings that he becomes a changed man, and to recover his true person he must undergo a penance that is both sentimental, or for love, and religious, for the salvation of his soul. That Amadís has reverted to a kind of psychological wilderness is evident in the way Montalvo has drawn in the figure of the holy hermit Andalod, who gives him the name Beltenebrós and takes him to the isolation of the Peña Pobre, and there oversees his physical and spiritual recovery.

Now in Cervantes' story both Cardenio and Don Quijote recall the crazed lover of sentimental romance who reverts to a wild state in a solitary landscape. [22] Their deranged behavior in Sierra Morena also recalls certain versions of the wild man legend. But while Cardenio's is the genuine case of a character deranged and driven to a wild state because of a treacherous outcome of his love affairs, Don Quijote's has to be the grand case of a love madness 'without cause' and hence conscious, reflective, gratuitous, the very conceit of a 'mad man imitating the mad knight' most deliberative from within his reasonings.

> —¿Ya no te he dicho ... que quiero imitar a Amadís, haciendo aquí del desesperado, del sandio y del furioso, por imitar juntamente al valiente don Roldán ... ?

> —Ahí está el punto ... y ésa es la fineza de mi negocio; que volverse loco un caballero andante con causa, ni grado ni gracias: el toque está desatinar sin ocasión y dar a entender a mi dama que, si en seco hago esto, ¿qué hiciera en mojado? I. 25

> —Have not I told thee already ... that I mean to follow Amadís, by playing here the despaired, wood, and furious man? To imitate likewise the valiant Orlando....

> —There is the point ... and therein consists the perfection of mine affairs; for that a knight-errant do run mad upon any just occasion deserves neither praise nor thanks; the wit is in waxing mad without cause, whereby my mistress may understand, that if dry I could do this, what would I have done being watered?

His love madness is 'without cause,' but not without purpose. He will undertake the rigors of a physical and spiritual penitent of love toward the end of acquiring "perpetual fame and renown," and in this way reach the "state of perfection of knighthood." He chooses to imitate Amadís and not Roland, because the former is the more sensitive lover, and his grief more delicate and feeling. [23] The wild setting of Sierra Morena becomes the solitary landscape of sentimental romance in the rapturous invocations to the sylvan beings of his imagination: "O ye Napeas and Dryads! which do wontedly inhabit the thickets and groves.... O solitary trees (which shall from henceforward keep company with my solitude), give tokens, with the soft motion of your boughs, that my presence doth not dislike you." I. 25. Here in a more profound way than in the adventures of the sheep flocks or the fullinghammers Don Quijote projects himself into a mythical role and time, because his imitation calls for a conscious reflection on his inward state. And hence he is able to maintain the illusion that his penance has lasted nearly as long as Amadís'.

The idea implicit in the parody of Beltenebrós is that he must be left alone to carry out his penance in isolation and solitude. Sancho is therefore sent away with a message to Dulcinea and he takes Rocinante with him, Dapple having disappeared. [24] Cervantes, following his bent for parody, has separated his characters, but he has also thought of Gandalín's grievous protests and entreaties as squire to Amadís, [25] and suggests them in Sancho's comical ones. A similar situation will arise when Don Quijote goes into the cave of Montesinos and is there permitted to live consummately and intimately the illusion of his knighthood. The letter to Dulcinea entrusted to Sancho is a parodic inversion of another kind; in Montalvo's version it is Oriana who writes vehement letters to her knight. In the summer of exemplary narrative Don Quijote's illusion of himself as a chosen knight is just that, and for the reader an illusion sustained by satirical effects. He is most lucid therefore precisely in these moments, when his illusion is most completely his own and he can call forth the unexampled gratuity of his actions. He imitates Amadís because he is the more logical and befitting model. Perhaps behind all this is the idea that his insanity, while turning inward toward the contemplation of himself as the subject of his sentimental reveries, is secretly wishing to be cured. And we know that the entire thrust of the exemplary story is toward an eventual cure:

after Don Quijote had ended his frisks and leaps, naked from the girdle downward, and from that upward apparelled, seeing that his squire Sancho was gone, and would behold no more of his mad pranks, he ascended to the top of a high rock, and began there to think on that whereon he had thought oftentimes before, without ever making a full resolution therein, to wit, whether were it better to imitate Orlando in his unmeasurable furies, than Amadís in his melancholy moods: and, speaking to himself, would say:

—If Orlando was so valorous and good a knight as men say, what wonder, seeing in fine he was enchanted, and could not be slain. . . . But, leaving his valour apart, let us come to the losing of his wits, which it is certain he lost through the signs he found in the forest, and by the news that the shepherd gave unto him, that Angelica had slept more than two noontides with the little Moor, Medoro. . . . But how can I imitate him in his furies, if I cannot imitate him in their occasion? for I dare swear for my Dulcinea of Toboso, that all the days of her life she hath not seen one Moor, even in his own attire as he is, and she is now right as her mother bore her; and I should do her a manifest wrong, if, upon any false suspicion, I should turn mad of that kind of folly that did distract furious Orlando. On the other side, I see that Amadís de Gaul, without losing his wits, or using any other raving trick, gained as great fame of being amorous as any one else whatsoever. . . . And this being true, as it is, why should I take now the pains to strip myself all naked, and offend these trees, which never yet did me any harm? Nor have I any reason to trouble the clear waters of these brooks, which must give me drink when I am thirsty. Let the remembrance of Amadís live, and be imitated in everything as much as may be, by Don Quijote of the Mancha; of whom may be said what was said of the other, that though he achieved not great things, yet did he die in their pursuit. And though I am not contemned or disdained by my Dulcinea, yet it is sufficient, as I have said already, that I be absent from her; therefore, hands to your task; and, ye famous actions of Amadís, occur to my remembrance, and instruct me where I may best begin to imitate you. Yet I know already, that the greatest thing he did use was prayer, and so will I. I. 26

The *Amadís* is romantic narrative where purely mythical elements have arrived at a characteristic transformation. Its geography, like its characters, is legendary and fabulous. The Poor Rock is a seagirt crag, isolated, inaccessible, except in summer, and here in a season and landscape of summer Beltenebrós was brought by the hermit who oversaw his penitence. Montalvo undoubtedly followed the outlines of the story taken from the Arthurian tradition that depicted the hero's emotional state against a landscape of summer fullness, sultry heat, heavy foliage and shady fountains. But, also, he framed the episode within the cyclical course of the seasons by placing its beginning at midsummer and ending it one year later on Saint John's Day. [26] As is usual in the Arthurian narratives, the action revolves around the dates of seasonal feasts, and the pattern of temporal duration is cast within their cyclical course, immutable from year to year. The emotional force of the story about Amadís' penance depends on his isolation, his breaking away from all dependence or comfort from his squire and companions. When Galaor and Florestán separated in order to carry out their search for him, they agreed to meet one year later at the court of King Lisuarte in London on Saint John's Day. The duration of their search was one year, but during that year and unknown to them, Amadís left the Poor Rock and was reunited with Oriana. Almost imperceptibly narrative duration moved forward to another year, and yet the reason remained constant. This temporal factor in the *Amadís* stands out in all its ingenuousness: In the due passage of time journeys are undergone and adventures undertaken, but the actual depiction of events is the season of a spring-like summer, immutable from year to year. This, as we shall see, is the story pattern that most likely influenced the temporal course of Don Quijote's adventures in Part Two.

In the summer of Part One the duality of Don Quijote, what he is and what he wants to be, is sustained fully across an exemplary span of time. And in the exemplary sense he is, at its close, no more than what he was at the start.

If he has become the famous knight and effectual hero it is only to himself, as part of the illusion and expectations his insanity provokes. The hoaxes played on him throughout the "Fourth Part," the succor of Princess Micomicoma, enchantments, prophecies, are intended primarily to get him home safely. Unlike the gratuitous and purely entertaining situations invented around him in Part Two, these have not the aura of his mythical fame in the real world as a starting point. The journey in the cart back to the village is lived by him as an enchantment laid on one of the chosen.

Although Don Quijote and Sancho find themselves back in their village much against their expectations, the force of their illusions remains intact. Don Quijote expects to become famous and Sancho expects to be rewarded with an island to govern. These have been the two 'mythical' motivations whose satirical and exemplary exposure set the story in motion and impelled it forward. As illusions they have to do with the resilience between motives and expectations. Thus Sancho's island is much less of an illusion acted out in all its literary consequences because he is more nearly the normal man and sensuous peasant than the image to himself of any squire or governor. After several weeks of adventures Sancho feels he has come closer to having his wish and goal, but since he has lived his 'mythical' illusion only as an expected reward, not as a radical transformation of his being, it is as near or as far as ever. In Part Two Sancho has also become famous, but fame has never been the desired or expected reward. From the start he has thought himself as deserving and able as the next to be made governor of an island. He has hardly thought of *becoming* worthier. The island is for him that magical reward never crucially contingent on his worth or exertions, or his ability to rule its inhabitants. On arrival back in the village Don Quijote is put to bed like a patient by his niece and housekeeper. He has already declared his mood and frame of mind about the course of events that have cut short his outing. When Sancho mentioned another sally "which may be more profitable and famous than this

hath been," he replied: "it will be a great wisdom to let
overpass the cross aspect of those planets that rein at this
present"; "y será gran prudencia dejar pasar el mal influjo
de las estrellas que agora corre." The final scene is Sancho's,
who is enlivened to speak to his wife of his ambitions:

> siendo Dios servido de que otra vez salgamos a viaje a buscar
> aventuras, vos me veréis presto conde, o gobernador de una ínsula,
> y no de las de por ahí, sino la mejor que pueda hallarse. I. 52
> *for and it please God that we travel once again to seek adventures,*
> *thou shalt see me shortly after an earl or governor of an island,*
> *and that not of every ordinary one neither, but of one of the best*
> *in the world. I. 52*

Sancho's island is his myth, so to speak, his mythical expectation to be made real in Part Two, in a way parallel to
Don Quijote's fame.

JUSTAS DE SAN JORGE: ZARAGOZA

In his 'mythical history' Alonso Quijano has not aged more
than a year (though he matures and develops in a way no
number of years could account for), from the onset of the
first summer to the close of the second. Although this
'mythical' lapse of time allowed him rests paradoxically on the
exemplary duration of the story, the narrative sense of both
is that they are thrust forward by a conception of narrative
time that is dynamic in its workings and prophetic in its
results. The illusions of the hidalgo and squire are held in
suspense at the close of Part One. Now, from the start, the
adventures of Part Two are pointed toward the spring festival
of Saint George. Now, unlike in the first two sallies, Don
Quijote sets out with a final destination in mind. But it has
been thought of by Carrasco, the harbinger of his fame
(see pp. 52 and 105 above).

"Justas de Zaragoza" were first mentioned at the close of
Part One as the crowning point of a third sally, and then
proposed by Carrasco in an opening scene of Part Two:

le respondió que era su parecer que fuese al reino de Aragón y a la
ciudad de Zaragoza, adonde *de allí a pocos días* se habían de hacer
unas solenísimas justas por la fiesta de San Jorge. II. 4

These jousts would be those held on or about the feastday
of Saint George (April 23), and from the onset they are imminent, "*. . . within a few days.*" [27] To travel from a village
in La Mancha to Zaragoza would require every one of several
days, and yet neither the hidalgo nor the author will feel
any compulsion to hurry there. The first episode is the visit
to El Toboso and the deception by Sancho presenting one
of the village girls to his master as Dulcinea (II. 10). The
vision of Dulcinea "enchanted" will become for its narrative
consequences the psychological reality that will hold sway
over the narrative duration of adventures in Part Two. Dulcinea enchanted is a vision outside chronological time; it is
an image of 'mythical' or 'magical' time. To disenchant her
will eventually become the pressing aim, and the measure of
success or failure. After the scene outside El Toboso knight
and squire remount,

y siguieron el camino de Zaragoza, adonde pensaban llegar a tiempo
que pudiesen hallarse en unas solenes fiestas que en aquella insigne
ciudad cada año suelen hacerse. Pero antes que allá llegasen, les
sucedieron cosas que, por muchas, grandes y nuevas, merecen ser
escritas, y leídas, como se verá adelante. II. 10

Arrival at Zaragoza is again stated as near. And this despite
the deferring of that arrival in the next sentence. But between
them both statements keep tense the immediacy of events.

After El Toboso, in the next series of adventures, they
swing east, and make a full turn south toward the Guadiana
and the cave of Montesinos. [28] They meet the cart of costumed
players, the Knight of the Mirrors, the Knight of the Green
Coat, the lions travelling in the cart, and then visit the home
of don Diego de Miranda. The season is spring, the scene is
festive, decorative, and akin to romantic pageantry. What
things are and what they appear to be is not a constant
shattering of the illusions of the hidalgo, but a similitude

of those illusions, exciting and saturating them. He triumphs in the world of action, but his ordeal and the sense of mission become contemplative, subjective.

Now, though the narrative gives an appearance of a forward and chronological movement, from the victory over the lion to arrival at the banks of the Ebro, in another sense this very movement is regressive, or recurrent, for each episode is actually occupying the same lapse of imaginary time. That is, each episode is occurring in the same interval, approaching or imminent to the jousts at Zaragoza. Temporal duration is imaginatively extended across successive episodes, while confined to a chronological interval that recurs for as many episodes as the author wishes to introduce. This has come about because of the one instigation to move towards Zaragoza (limitation) for a specific occasion, and the other to develop to the full (extension) the course of adventitious adventure. Their workings are mutual, not contradictory. And least of all in the question of distances covered, so confusing to Cervantes' chronologers. The course of adventures must provide for the "enlargement" of the hero; it is therefore protracted, extended in time and space. The process of enlargement, as we shall see presently, casts the hero's psychological attributes against a mythical delineation. For this a nearly unrestricted narrative duration is mandatory, but a duration that must yet be confined to the seasonal interval just preceding jousts at Zaragoza. Although this interval was mentioned as brief at the onset (II. 10, II. 18), it is subsequently said to be extended and then is finally suspended as indefinite (II. 27). The subsequent course of the story, from the descent into the cave of Montesinos to the flight on Clavileño, is determined by the process of enlargement and not by any observance of dates and distances covered.

Thus, when Don Quijote and Sancho prepare to leave Don Diego's home, and though their "straight-line" destination is Zaragoza, they set out for a round of adventures in the immediate vicinity: "donde esperaba entretener el tiempo *hasta que llegase el día de las justas de Zaragoza, que era el de su derecha derrota;* y que primero había de entrar en la cueva de Montesinos" (II. 18). While each adventure is developed within its narrative interval, it does not follow that chronological time has advanced. These episodes are taking place on a recurrent span of time. Each one ensuing preempts and therefore succeeds to the span of time of its predecessor. As Cervantes conceives and thereon develops them he gives to each the same "realistic" chronological interval. In his mind each episode is occupying the same interval of imaginary time, the spring period leading up to the festival of Saint George at Zaragoza. 'Episodic time' we might call it, for while the narrative is not moving forward in natural or chronological time within the passage of days and hours, each episode is nevertheless completing by degrees the mythical delineation of the mock hero. Given the end and results, as well as the means, can we provide a source or preconception for this procedure? Yes. Cervantes, while proceeding with a temporal outline adequate to his ends, was in fact adumbrating the romantic story pattern of a spring-like summer as the season and landscape for chivalric adventure. But what is even more surprising is that, having provided initially a feastday in spring as the immediate goal, he then arrested or protracted the entire course of adventures within a relatively short period, thus fitting his narrative pattern into the arc of spring festivals in the solar cycle. Moreover, out of the story pattern, and in direct contrast to it, there emerges an entirely new conception of narrative time that we like to think of as congenial to the novel, whereby the development of character may proceed on a temporal pattern entirely its own, and independent of concern for chronological order or form. The very conception of Don Quijote *dilatado* (enlarged) called for a temporal design pre-eminent to a verisimilar chronology.

Between the departure from Don Diego's home and arrival at the banks of the Ebro, we have the episodes of Camacho's [*sic*] wedding, the descent into the cave of Montesinos, the episode at the inn and Master Peter's puppet show, then the braying adventure. Upon leaving the inn, where he pays material damages for wrecking the puppets, the knight and his squire set off for the river: "determinó de ver primero las riberas del río Ebro y todos aquellos contornos antes de entrar en la ciudad de Zaragoza, *pues le daba tiempo para todo el mucho que faltaba desde allí a las justas*" II. 27. The intention will now be for the knight to linger and for the author to delay or suspend arrival and entry into Zaragoza almost indefinitely. As we noted at the beginning of our study, by Don Quijote's count twenty-seven days elapsed between the day they set out for their village and their arrival on the banks of the Ebro; "veinte y cinco días ha que salimos de nuestro pueblo...." II. 28; "dos días después que salieron de la alameda llegaron don Quijote y Sancho al río Ebro...." II. 29. After nearly a month on the road, jousts in Zaragoza are still forthcoming, not within a few days as at the start of the sally, but within a date that now recedes indefinitely. Apparently, as they move closer to the Ebro the proximity of the date for jousts at Zaragoza fades away. Moreover, as they move north from the Guadiana after the cave episode, Don Quijote's adventures have become less positive, less decisive, in a material sense. By comparison with the puppet play, the braying adventure, and the enchanted bark, the episode of the lion was a triumph of the spirit over matter. By degrees Cervantes has prepared the stage for the prolonged stay at the ducal palace, where, at the expense of his freedom, the knight's heroic image of himself will be amply confirmed. Accordingly, jousts at Zaragoza will not be mentioned again until the end of that stay, in Chapter 52. Then knight and squire set out for Zaragoza at the close of Chapter 57. The very next adventure is the episode of a fanciful and feigned Arcadia, and the scene and occasion will again suggest late spring or incipient summer, although according to events just narrated it should be late August or September.

Thus, as Chapter 52 opens, jousts at Zaragoza are again imminent, and once again the date in April is presumable for them.

Cuenta Cide Hamete que estando ya don Quijote sano de sus aruños, le pareció que la vida que en aquel castillo tenía era contra toda la orden de caballería que profesaba, y así, determinó de pedir licencia a los duques para partirse *a Zaragoza, cuyas fiestas llegaban cerca,* adonde pensaba ganar el arnés que en tales fiestas se conquista.

MYTHICAL TIME: DESCENT AND FLIGHT

Sabed que tenéis aquí en vuestra presencia ... aquel gran caballero de quien tantas cosas tiene profetizadas el sabio Merlín: aquel don Quijote de la Mancha, digo, que de nuevo y con mayores ventajas que en los pasados siglos ha resucitado en los presentes la ya olvidada andante caballería, por cuyo medio y favor podría ser que nosotros fuésemos desencantados; que las grandes hazañas para los grandes hombres están guardadas. II. 23

Know that you have here in your presence ... that famous knight of whom Merlin prophesied such great matters, that Don Quijote de la Mancha, I say, that now newly, and more happily than former ages, hath raised the long-forgotten knight-errantry, by whose means and favour it may be that we also may be disenchanted; for great exploits are reserved for great personages.

In the adventure of the cave Montesinos addresses the prostrate Durandarte. It is the great and moving scene for Don Quijote, for in this vision he moves as an equal among the shades of heroic chivalry. [29] Is he the knight for whom this great feat of deliverance has been reserved? This adventure is framed from beginning to end as one great, but bipartite, interrogation: is it a vision or reality? And: is he the knight harbored in the depths of time for this stupendous feat? In the depths of the reply there lies another question: he is that knight — if he has indeed the virtue to enact, to empower it. But indirectly, and in a most disarming way, the vision of himself in the cave reveals Don Quijote's deepest insufficiency, his impotence. I refer to his inability to lend Dulcinea the full six reales she needs. If the descent into the cave is the symbolic descent into the subconscious, Don Quijote prefigures his own admission of failure. Montesinos' instructions on just how Don Quijote can break the spell of centuries remain indiscernible. But his presence in the cave

alone makes that event imminent. Yet the cave experience
prefigures the outcome of his insufficiency to disenchant
Dulcinea in the world above. He comes before Montesinos
as the knight from the historical world who can break the
spell that holds knighthood enthralled. But he will leave
the cave burdened with the personal image of Dulcinea
enchanted and the memory of his inability to remedy her need.

When the hidalgo first conceived the renewal of chivalry
as his enterprise he fell into a misconception that the exemplary story has exposed at every turn. This misconception
was that chivalric accounts were historical, and that their
heroes had been, all of them, men of "flesh and bone." Hence
a man like himself of flesh and bone could revive their
efforts, and in doing so remake himself in their image. In
order to sustain this quixotic idea the misconception must be
lived to the full, as a propitious incentive, with goals realizable
almost immediately. Nowhere was this better explained than
by Don Quijote himself in the conversation with the canon
in Chapter 50 of Part One. Subsequently, in the opening
conversations of Part Two he reaffirmed his desire to restore
in the present the golden age of chivalry, advancing it as a
utopian solution to the menace of the Turk and even to social
ills, thereby exposing the whole idea as another misconception
of history. Or, rather, of what is antiquated by history and
thereby rendered ineffectual. All of which goes to say that
for Don Quijote, in matters chivalric, there are no distinctions
between myths, romance, or history, or between fiction and
reality; these are one and the same when seen in terms of
valor, personal enterprise, and incentive. And he could not
accept what happened to him in the cave as a dream. Hence
no distinctions exist between himself and the heroes of
chivalry, whether historical or romantic. It is sufficient for
him to desire passionately to be like them to be made equal
to them. He is unable to see that Amadís was never obsessed
with the goal of acquiring fame because that obsession is
never a part of his literary world. Amadís' fame is a generic
feature of his literary figuration, like his invincibility or his

marvelous birth. But Don Quijote's obsession is to find in the world of sense experience the confirmation of what is only an image of himself: his fame, as evidence of his effectuality, as the proof of his valor and virtue. This, then, is what is at stake in the visionary adventure of the cave.

What he finds in the underworld as the condition of chivalry confirms his view of it in the world above. Montesinos, Durandarte, Belerma, and who knows how many other knights and ladies, are held in the grip of an enchantment. The "flesh and bone" figures of chivalry are imprisoned in time, or, rather, in age. They live on quiescent, in a death-like duration. The ages have worked their corrosive effects on the bodies of these famous who cannot die, most perversely on the beauty of Belerma's features. It is the nature of the spell to suspend sequential time, but not durational time. The enchantment will go on forever, until the one elected being capable of breaking it intervenes. This underworld is a reflection of the world above, and both are subject to the laws of necessity in an age of iron. But in the cave the belief and resolve that sustain Don Quijote in the world above are reflected as doubt and perplexity. Is he the knight who will break the spell of historical time? Is it true that Montesinos took out Durandarte's heart with a small dagger ... one perhaps resembling a surgical instrument? [30] It *did* occur to him to ask this question. It did not occur to him to ask why these persons were enchanted in just a stage of incident and circumstance, the state precisely of their "fame," — Durandarte alive and on the catafalque, but without a heart; — the heart delivered to Belerma and preserved, not marvelously, as one might expect, by magic, but withered, under the effects of age. The complete picture is such that one concludes that it answers to the mission that Don Quijote has set for himself. Yet the deepest revelations concern the feelings he has of powerlessness, of an overwhelming concentration on the details of the vision and the challenge, and yet the sense of being powerless to meet it.

The enchantments Don Quijote confronts are, among other things, both the adverse forces his virtue and skill must overcome and, but secretly, the testament of his fame. Enchantments have the power to disorder and suspend the natural and rational course of things. They are to themselves a different order of time. And his fame is as much of that order as of any other. His fame can be 'mythical' because it belongs as much to the 'magical time' of enchantments as to the moral order of his reasons for reviving chivalry. The reflections of the cave's distorted world make clear that Don Quijote's thrust for fame is the element that suspends and resolves all the different orders of time in which he is depicted, historical, romantic, or 'magical.'

Like the image of Dulcinea, the fame of Don Quijote is one of the great structural fictions of Cervantes' innovation. Thus, just as the mock hero is unable to see that Amadís' fame is a fiction operative in the actual world, for to him it is as real as the fame of any famous man who truly lived, so too does Don Quijote remain throughout his book supremely unaware of the fictional (fraudulent) nature of his own fame. For us the adventure of the cave is a fiction of several levels, but for the character it must be a whole truth. Yet clearly the adventure in the cave as told by him is the prototype of the quixotic fiction, because it is the hero himself who tells it. And since it is a fiction within a fiction, it evolves in a time within a time, each with its corresponding duration. Sancho is shocked to hear that it lasted throughout three days and nights because he knows his master was in the cave for only a little over half an hour. But the question of a fictional time in the cave is really the question of Don Quijote's fame, because that fame is here suspended in a 'mythical' time that dissolves all his temporal misconceptions, in a present here-and-now fraught with possibilities.

Now the prototypal chivalric fiction is a test, quest, or deed of deliverance that breaks the evil spell cast on an entire kingdom. Of course this fiction is mythical, because it is not subject to the sequence or duration of any other order or

conception of time, exemplary, historical, or natural. The time
of this fiction is based on these orders, yes, but the act of
deliverance implies that the hero can penetrate into the
magical time and power of the spell and break it, and return
to the historical or natural world a moral and mythical
champion. This is exactly what Don Quijote accomplishes on
the flying horse Clavileño, and as told by Cervantes this
adventure is the counterpart of the vision in the cave. Everything about these two adventures is 'fictional,' but they confirm
the knight's image of himself as a mythic hero.

However, there is one adventure that takes place between
them that is as revelatory as they are of Don Quijote's mythical time. I refer to the puppet play, the story of Melisendra's
rescue by Gaiferos. Of all the chivalric stories Cervantes wove
into his own this one has provided the only successfully
completed rescue of a lady by a knight in the entire book. Of
course it has to be presented as a pure fiction, with a poetic
duration and sequence of its own, and framed by the orders
of an exemplary time and place in the inn, with an audience
that includes the hidalgo. Cervantes' formula is evident, however unconsciously he traced it: the greater the degree of
execution and effectuality on the part of the knight, the more
completely the whole is delivered to the reader or spectator,
including the hidalgo, as a fiction. In the presence of Don
Quijote, a puppet knight mounted on a puppet horse performs
the kind of rescue of an abducted lady that could conceivably
free Dulcinea. Master Peter's puppets enact a romance, and
at the moment when their flight is most endangered, Don
Quijote breaks onto the stage and in a splendid, gratuitous
act of bravery ensures their escape. They would have escaped
in any case, according to the story. Why, then, did Don
Quijote intervene? Is there a 'fictional' explanation for his
irrational act? Assuredly there is. Don Quijote breaks in on
the scene because the danger to the fleeing couple is, for
him, frightfully real. He has not been so much a witness in
fact to the play as a participant in spirit. For him their escape
is taking place in a 'mythical' time and is vivid in sense

experience. [31] He intervenes and slashes at the moorish puppets in order to prove himself the efficacious agent of a mythical escape.

The puppet stage is a miniature of the historical world, where Don Quijote can perform a gratuitous rescue on a grand scale. But the world of enchantments in the cave confronts the knight with a quest shaped to bitter necessity, one he cannot fail to attempt, the quest most subtly confronted in the vision of Dulcinea enchanted. As the subsequent course of the story proves, her disenchantment is the major theme that unifies the episodic plot to its close. In Dulcinea's enchantment Cervantes adumbrated the other great theme of chivalric lore, the abduction of the lady and her rescue, precisely the theme of the Lancelot-Guenievre story as conceived by Chrétien. Derived from mythological tales of the seasonal abduction of a vegetation goddess or bride, the romantic theme portrays the abductor as an analogue of the forces of winter and prince of 'the land from whence no one returns.' So much for romance, for, in the novel we know as *Don Quijote,* the 'abduction' and enchantment of Dulcinea has become a psychological fiction. And by this fiction, is not Dulcinea 'abducted' and held 'enchanted' by time itself? That is, by time out-of-time, and out of the reach of the knight's effectualness?

In Don Quijote's conviction, Dulcinea's enchantment becomes as inexplicable as it is inflexible. In his vision of her in the cave she is under a spell in the other world along with the other figures of chivalry. This same spell looms over the conditions subsequently imposed for her disenchantment, for the knight is all but powerless to bring it about. But the psychological abduction, so to speak, inflicts the greater injury to his vision of himself as her knight, for, from the scene on the outskirts of El Toboso to her appearance on the wagon beside Merlin (II. 35), she no longer belongs to him as an intimate and idealized being. It is significant that in the vision of the cave, Guenievre, along with Quintañona, is under the same enigmatic enchantment in an inaccessible region.

As if to heighten their imprint on the senses, the adventures in the cave and the flight on Clavileño are the two in the book where Don Quijote does not directly see what is before him. In the first we are to assume that his eyes are closed in sleep. In the other he rides aloft blindfolded. In this way at least their fictional nature is concealed from him. As adventures they are configured for him and imagined by him across time and space on a grand scale. They trace the two great archetypal movements of the human soul in search of freedom. But the cave is clearly a descent into time, and the ride on Clavileño is an ascent into and across space. The deliverance of the Countess Trifaldi, Antonomasia, Don Clavijo, and the bearded dueñas, is accomplished almost timelessly, across vast spaces. As a fiction whose meaning is precisely that it is accomplished in mythical time, it is the one unequivocal feat carried out by the mock knight. It makes evident that Don Quijote's mythical effectuality is one and the same with his fame, for according to Malambruno's conditions, it is sufficient that so famous and valorous a knight merely undertakes this feat to bring it to a triumphant close:

> El ínclito caballero don Quijote de la Mancha feneció y acabó la aventura de la Condesa Trifaldi, por otro nombre llamada la dueña Dolorida, y compañía, *con sólo intentarla.* II. 41
>
> *The famous and valorous knight Don Quijote de la Mancha finished and ended the adventure of the Countess Trifaldi, otherwise called the afflicted dame, and her company,* only with undertaking it. *II. 41*

Here is formal notice that the consummation of Don Quijote's illusion of his effectuality belongs to mythical time. His illusion has been sustained throughout his adventures by the imminence of just such a consummation as this, and the recognition that it bestows: "el duque ... con los brazos abiertos, fue a abrazar a don Quijote, diciéndole ser el más buen caballero que en ningún siglo se hubiese visto"; "and straight with open arms the duke went to embrace Don Quijote, telling him he was the bravest knight that ever was."

The withered heart and the grisly beards are minuscle configurations of temporal processes of natural laws behind the challenge laid down by the enchantments. So far as these enchantments are the work of supernatural powers, Don Quijote's foreseeable triumph over them looms magnificent. As a fiction conceived by his own mind and sensibility the enchantment in the cave with its relationship between cause and effect is instructive. The two groups of enchanted victims combined are a picture of a fallen humanity, in need of the intercession of a deliverer. But the enchantment in the cave is inexplicable as an effect with a cause. What reason did Merlin have to inflict this enchantment that has lasted for over five hundred years? What transgression, if any, did Montesinos, Durandarte, or Belerma commit? Why have they drawn the ill will of the formidable enchanter? Such matters defy an explanation; they are a part of the vast interrogation and enigma of the cave. As a fiction spun to Don Quijote's illusions about himself, the mayordomo's story is by contrast precise in its cause and consequences. The bearded dueñas are a picture of pathetic humanity in the grips of a punishment adequate to their unrestrained sensuality. [32] That bearded men have impersonated them hints at a failing common to both sexes. The cause of the enchantment has been the moral failing of Countess Trifaldi as a dueña; due to her sensuality she allowed Antonomasia to be seduced. In the society of Cervantes' time a man's honor and virility were attached to his beard; in the quixotic transposition beards on dueñas are a sign of self-inflicted dishonor.

These quixotic enchantments have ultimately to do not with the power of magic over natural or moral law, but with the relative powerlessness of magic over natural processes. The heart will continue to wither, for no amount of preservatives can defraud the natural process, though it probably will not be reduced to dust. The beards on dueñas are against nature, certainly, but not against the law that ordains that once sprouted there they must continue to grow, and frightfully in the heat of summer. Don Quijote is effectual as a fictional knight against supernatural powers, but how effective can he be against merely natural ones? Though the magic operative in these enchantments makes it apparent that what Don Quijote faces are supernatural powers, these he can overcome; natural powers, like those that sustain the fleshy organism that is Sancho's body, or the aging process, are as insurmountable as ever. Thus, though embedded in the mythical time of Don Quijote's illusion, these two challenges are configured ultimately in the exemplary process that encloses the life span of the hidalgo. A heart turning to dust or a brushy hair growth are minute processes of the law of growth, death, and decay. According to this law, the life span of any man is a linear movement, irreversible and finite, and hence unique.

SAINT JOHN'S DAY: BARCELONA

When Cervantes substituted Barcelona for Zaragoza as the final destination for the third sally he was recasting not just an old plan, but the very substance of his narrative. The long stay at the ducal palace allowed Don Quijote and Sancho to pursue their illusions and expectations to their eventful and separate disillusionments. Having postponed their departure for week after week, the summer of chivalric illusion was fulfilled amidst the pomp and display of a magnificent palace and on a veritable island, seemingly isolated from the currents of historical time. Here the passage of time seemed all but imperceptible, even as narrative duration moved forward along an exemplary course into July and August. Thus, the shape of illusion fulfilled is time seemingly immutable or suspended, a consequence of that binary movement that gives us a mythical delineation across an exemplary span.

We have seen how the prospect of arrival at Zaragoza in time for the jousts of Saint George induced a recurrence of narrative intervals within a period imminent to these festivities. Now we may consider that in the narrative duration of the sojourn at the palace an interval amounting to an entire solar year has gone by, so that when Don Quijote and Sancho set out for Barcelona in Chapter 59 narrative time is again spring, in order to sustain as imminent the seasonal festival that will crown Don Quijote's career. We are now in a position to see that this recurrent movement corresponds to the cyclical, mythical story pattern of romance. Narrative duration moves forward according to the natural and exemplary sequence, but the season reverts (or moves forward) to spring and the advent of summer in a cyclical movement. We have an advance in exemplary duration and a recurrence that conforms to a mythical pattern. The season and with it narrative time is again spring, in order to sustain as imminent the hour of fulfilment of Don Quijote's illusion about his fame, and about what his arrival and welcome at his destination should be. In other words, this situation is called for by the demands of parody. Yet Cervantes actually brought his mock hero onto a stage where his triumph is shortlived and his disillusion and defeat forthcoming.

In phase three of Part Two the fictional hero has moved onto the stage of history. This has been a consequence of both the developing structure of his depictment within the book and the success of his book in the historical world of 1605-1614. The renown of an authentic Don Quijote in the real world is the fact reflected in the fiction and recreated there as one of his mythical attributes. Cervantes was undoubtedly provoked into taking his story in this direction by Avellaneda's imitation, for now to prove that his character is the genuine Don Quijote the author must demonstrate the reality of his character as his fictional creation. From the time he leaves the inn in Chapter 59 Don Quijote assumes his new and final configuration. His fame in the real or historical world is the fictional distortion of the true image of himself that has sustained him through trials, anxieties, and humiliations. Exposed now to the reality of the historical world, his ordeal is to maintain that heroic image of himself in an affliction of the spirit. Which is to say that the process by which his chivalric role is turned inward is by now all but complete. Hence those rash or violent attacks to prove his valor or identity have been obviated. He meets everywhere with evidence of his success, and this recognition is sufficient as an adventure. And from the start of this final phase Cervantes has contrasted his fictional hero with a genuine hero of history, Roque Guinart. In this final phase he introduced from the historical scene of 1610-1614 matters relating to the expulsion of the moriscos, civil strife and banditry in Catalonia, and the naval menace of the Turk. In none of these matters is Don Quijote pressed to prove his effectuality; for his chivalric role is now outwardly ceremonial and inwardly meditative. Roque, by comparison, is the dynamic historical hero who surmounts danger instinctively, who imposes his will by bloodshed and violence. Events in Roque's life are tragic and real, not burlesque; and so they are in the life of Ricote the morisco and his daughter. These historical figures and events enlarge in one sweep the fiction of Don Quijote. They give him an historical configuration within the book, though they are the actors and he is the spectator of these 'historical' fictions, yet they are enclosed within them, whereas Don Quijote being fictional has become mythical. Thus, as Don Quijote and Sancho move toward Barcelona in the company of Roque, they move toward the historical moment of 1614 that will complete the mock hero's delineation amidst the life of the city and the sea. So intent was Cervantes on making his fiction conform to his knowledge of historical conditions that Don Quijote must make his way to Barcelona under the protection of the real-life bandit who assaulted travellers and held the countryside subject to him. [33]

En fin, por caminos desusados, por atajos y sendas encubiertas, partieron Roque, don Quijote y Sancho con otros seis escuderos a Barcelona. Llegaron a su playa la víspera de San Juan en la noche. ...

Volvióse Roque; quedóse don Quijote esperando el día, así, a caballo, como estaba, y no tardó mucho cuando comenzó a descubrirse por los balcones del Oriente la faz de la blanca aurora, alegrando las yerbas y las flores, en lugar de alegrar el oído; aunque al mesmo instante alegraron también el oído el son de muchas chirimías y atabales, ruido de cascabeles, "¡trapa, trapa, aparta, aparta!" de corredores, que, al parecer, de la ciudad salían. Dio lugar la aurora al sol, que, un rostro mayor que el de una rodela, por el más bajo horizonte poco a poco se iba levantando.

Tendieron don Quijote y Sancho la vista por todas partes: vieron el mar, hasta entonces dellos no visto; parecióles espaciosísimo y largo, harto más que las lagunas de Ruidera ... ; vieron las galeras que estaban en la playa, las cuales, abatiendo las tiendas, se descubrieron llenas de flámulas y gallardetes, que tremolaban al viento y besaban y barrían el agua; dentro sonaban clarines, trompetas y chirimías, que cerca y lejos llevaban el aire de suaves y belicosos acentos. II. 61

The trajectory and space-time relationship that brings Don Quijote for all time onto the stage of history could not be more complete. His arrival is on the morning of Saint John's Day because like the sun at midsummer he reaches the highest point on the arc of an ascending career. His entry into the city is the grand but fleeting hour of apotheosis, and a few days later his defeat beside the sea is the dark hour that begins his decline and the return of his steps homeward, to disillusion and death.

Saint John's Day in chivalric romances is an occasion for solemn religious rituals, for social and courtly processions, for tourneys and folk festivals, both serious and playful, with a long tradition in aristocratic and popular practices, and, moreover, the climax of spring festivals that beginning with the spring equinox (Easter) celebrate the consummation of the solar year. [34] Don Quijote's entry into the great port city of Barcelona is a burlesque imitation of numerous scenes of pageantry in the *Amadís* and other romances on a date reserved for the most solemn commemorations. His arrival and reception are of course in the spirit of the burlesque festivities on the surface of the parodic coincidence as well as in the depths of an exemplary art. The entire series of scenes is lived by him inwardly as a spectacle unfolding directly out of the many ceremonial and festive rituals celebrated on Saint John's Day in chivalric romances. The mythical illusion is complete, and the satiety of the senses is the hero's hold on the situation around him, for he moves about these festivities like a ceremonial figure. His arrival at sunrise, coincident with the advent of summer, underscores their significance as the consummation of the season of romance, of the fulness of time, and the promise of perpetual fame. In this hour of triumph, who would suppose he was not invincible?

The course of adventures northward has seen the grand trajectory of the hero advance toward the consummation of his fame and the mythical hour of triumph and apotheosis. As such his adventures have taken on progressively a decorative, processional and ceremonial aspect, duly climaxed with the description of the sunrise over the sea, and his entry into the city. But because his fame has preceded him to this hour, his progress from the cave of Montesinos to Barcelona has brought him to this scene of welcome and acclaim, the final fulfilment of mythical renown that time has held prophetically in store for him. The illusion, overwhelmingly confirmed by the color, the shouts and music, is complete. From the sunrise over the sea to the showy and noisy entry into the city he is once more the silent and passive observer. The fame of Don Quijote has preceded him to this hour of triumph; the natural creation and its lord the sun acclaim him. The cheers of the city's teeming populace are an acknowledgement of his fame. Hence the occasion resembles and even reflects the scene of welcome in the cave:

—Bien sea venido a nuestra ciudad el espejo, el farol, la estrella y el norte de toda la caballería andante. ... II. 61

Don Antonio Moreno ... andaba buscando modos como, sin su perjuicio, sacase a plaza sus locuras. ... Lo primero que hizo fue ... sacarle ... a un balcón que salía a una calle de las más principales de la ciudad, a vista de las gentes y de los muchachos, que como a mona le miraban. Corrieron de nuevo delante dél los de las libreas, como si para él solo, no para alegrar aquel festivo día, se las hubieran puesto.

Comieron aquel día con don Antonio algunos de sus amigos, honrando todos y tratando a don Quijote como a caballero andante, de lo cual, hueco y pomposo, no cabía en sí de contento. II. 62

> *Don Antonio Moreno ... began to invent, how, without prejudice to him, he might divulge his madness ... so he brought him to a balcony which looked toward one of the chiefest streets in the city, to be publicly seen by all comers, and the boys that beheld him as if he had been a monkey. They in the liveries began afresh to fetch careers before him, as if for him only (and not to solemnize that festival day) their liveries had been put on.*

> *That day some of Don Antonio's friends dined with him, all honouring Don Quijote, and observing him as a knight errant: with which, being most vain-glorious, he could scarce contain himself in his happiness. II. 62*

When the Knight of the White Moon points his lance at Don Quijote's visor and forces him to admit defeat and accept the humiliation of an enforced retirement for the length of a year, he is imitating a chivalric practice derived from the ritual combats of a solar mythology. The two mock antagonists have engaged in combat at midsummer like two surrogates of celestial and seasonal divinities who wage an annual recurring combat in myths. In the cyclical course of solar time the young sun god will replace the old, as a mythical conception, but in the exemplary course of Don Quijote's lifetime there will be no recurrence and no recovery. But if the mock knight follows the course of sun gods and solar heroes to mock triumph and apotheosis, this turning point that marks his defeat is also decisive as the initial point of his subsequent mythical figuration as we know him in historical time. The dejected knight who retraces his steps back to La Mancha is Alonso Quijano who dies a sane man. Defeat and humiliation become the symbolical act by which Don Quijote fails and falls, but to rise thereon as a Christ of fiction. [35] From the moment of his defeat Don Quijote belongs, as a martyred figure of fiction, to historical time. The very momentum of his story had led Cervantes to depict his mock hero defeated in an historical moment and setting. He had in fact been induced to this by the notoriety and fame his character had acquired by the year 1615. But by depicting his character as the entertaining mock hero his contemporaries joked and talked about he was now in fact supplying the condition that would insure a mythical figuration for his character in time to come. His is perhaps the only character of fiction who, in his own book, moves out of a 'fictional' delineation onto the stage of history and on this stage, in view of the world and the reading public, is defeated, in a mock battle. At this turning point, I would say, Don Quijote and Cervantes parted ways.

CONCLUSION

Pensar que en esta vida las cosas della han de durar siempre en un estado, es pensar en lo escusado; antes parece que ella anda todo en redondo, digo, a la redonda: la primavera sigue al verano, el verano al estío, el estío al otoño, y el otoño al invierno, y el invierno a la primavera, y así torna a andarse el tiempo con esta rueda continua; sola la vida humana corre a su fin ligera más que el tiempo, sin esperar renovarse si no es en la otra, que no tiene términos que la limiten. Esto dice Cide Hamete, filósofo mahomético; porque esto de entender la ligereza e inestabilidad de la vida presente, y la duración de la eterna que se espera, muchos sin lumbre de fe, sino con la luz natural, lo han entendido; pero aquí nuestro autor lo dice por la presteza con que se acabó, se consumió, se deshizo, se fue como en sombra y humo el gobierno de Sancho. II. 53

To think that the affairs of this life should last ever in one being is needless; for it rather seems otherwise; the summer follows the spring; after the summer, the fall; and the fall, the winter; and so time goes on in a continued wheel. Only man's life runs to a speedy end, swifter than time, without hope of being renewed, except it be in another life, which hath no bounds to limit it. This said Cide Hamete, a Mahometical philosopher; for many, without the light of faith, only with a natural instinct, have understood the swiftness and uncertainty of this life present, and the lasting of the eternal life which is expected. But here the author speaks it for the speediness with which Sancho's government was ended, consumed, and undone, and vanished into a shade and smoke. II. 53

We may close by first observing that Cide Hamete in the passage above has described the two most prominent conceptions of time in modern civilization: the cyclical, in the image of the wheel, and the linear, with the allusion to life's brevity that recalls Góngora's image of the arrow (in the

sonnet "Menos solicitó veloz saeta..."). But the conception
of the wheel has necessarily included the cyclical pattern of
the natural course of the seasons and with it the idea that
natural time revolves and that situations may recur, but
that the life span of individuals is finite and mortal. Sancho's
rule over Barataria vanishes like smoke, and like smoke
dispersed by the wind it seemed to Sancho that his master's
glory and promises to him died when he saw him fall and
admit defeat to the Knight of the White Moon. The temporality, and hence brevity, of life is the general theme that
encompasses the life and death of illusions, and even of
material objects. Experienced and conceived as a duration
and continuous flow, the course of life seems assured, and
from such assurance arise those illusions that impel a given
individual to fame, to enterprise, to selfless sacrifice, and so
the end of life must come as unexpected, and what was real
and solid while it lasted must appear when vanished fleeting and vain.

Yet our passage above leads to another concept of time,
but one out-of-time and not merely time*less*, the eternal. This
concept is beyond the bounds of this study, however, for it
lies outside of Cervantes' story. Or, rather, it comes into play
only now, as the story closes.

> Como las cosas humanas no sean eternas, yendo siempre en
> declinación de sus principios hasta llegar a su último fin, especial-
> mente las vidas de los hombres, y como la de don Quijote no tuviese
> privilegio del cielo para detener el curso de la suya, llegó su fin y
> acabamiento cuando él menos lo pensaba; porque, o ya fuese de la
> melancolía que le causaba el verse vencido, o ya por la disposición
> del cielo, que así lo ordenaba, se le arraigó una calentura, que le
> tuvo seis días en la cama. II. 74

His death comes to him unexpected, and yet it was implicit
from the start in the exemplary plan. According to this plan
the course of madness is spent in freedom and exhilaration
for the body, the mind and the imagination, but once spent
there is no simple return to health and sanity, for these may
be regained only through mortal admission of error and

repentance. Don Quijote's final phase is the luminosity of conscience revealed by Alonso Quijano in his final hours. He regains the inner light of health and peace, he renounces the romances of chivalry, in an exemplary admission of error and *desengaño,* but seemingly as a consequence he must die, as an act obedient to nature, and to the poetic justice underlying an exemplary story. Inwardly illuminated as to his error, yet his is not an exemplary 'religious' death. One may say with more truth that it is 'secular.' Alonso Quijano dies a natural death so that the mythical renown of Don Quijote may live on in historical time, dislodged before us from the mortal body of the character who dies. Thus the binary movement and configuration of time sweeps outward from the fiction of the book to fictionalize the historical world of Cervantes' readers.

The time-shape of such a book is at once a contrast and the mutual reflection upon the other of a "naive" or timeless conception of story-telling and a "critical" or rationalist art of narration. And Cervantes is of course both "naive" and "critical," and most baffling when we consider that his "critical" side is applied to reducing the marvelous element of medieval tales to an exemplary formula whilst his "naive" side fabricates the pluralistic structure of the modern novel. Such a book is all-important in literary history, and yet its importance is that it defies classifications of an historical nature (Renaissance, Baroque, etc.).

Take for example the whole theme of Don Quijote's thrust for fame. This theme is perfectly explicable as a dynamic and inward re-working (psychological and subjective according to the mock knight's characterization) of personal glory and aggrandizement that we find in Castilian literature of the fifteenth century. We can trace every element of this theme to its antecedents in the idea of "secular" fame. And we can analyze each of those elements in the psychology of Don Quijote's distraught but exalted imagination and the morality of his actions, and illustrate thereby some dogmatic currents of the Counter Reformation. But in the process we shall find that the fame of Don Quijote as an incentive and a fiction is a timeless story of his actions and illusions, sustained without reference to rules of art or dogmas of belief. A comical book of romantic adventures closes with the serious and even tragic death scene, contrary again to the patterns of either romance, comedy, or epic. Such an ending is the consequence of the complete absorption of romantic elements into an exemplary story by an author at once "critical" and "naive." The binary movement of time across the story in two Parts is a consequence of the projection, from the start, of an exemplary story toward its fanciful consummation (and hence also distortion, since the means are parody and satire) in chivalric myth. From our critical point of view they are both a literary time, or a literary configuration of time. By this I mean that the realistic and historical basis of the story is not less a literary configuration than the poetic and mythical elements that constitute Don Quijote's imaginary world and impel his illusion.

Just as the quixotic fiction is built of fictions within fictions, so likewise is the configuration of time one of lesser configurations within the two major movements. And within the lesser configurations we find smaller units of narrative time, down to the scale of the minute and the minuscule. The two major configurations are the *exemplary* and the *romantic,* corresponding to the two principal conceptions of our analysis, the psychological (*humor,* psychosis, etc.) and the mythical. And within the large-scale movements of the major configurations we have described various orders of time at work, and no episode or theme of the book can be understood simply in terms of chronology and duration. Take for example the question of wages to be paid Sancho. One would think that a sum of money and a calculable amount of time could be arrived at, but such is not the case, for ultimately the span of time that Sancho works for wages, and their computable worth in coinage, is to be "configured" within one or more fictional times. The *exemplary* describes the course of the three sallies in natural time and contains

the portraits of the principal characters and the process of
their characterization. It is also of course the temporal form
for the moral truth of their lives. It forms the basis for any
conception of the story, or novel, as a process, whether of an
unfolding of a psychological aberration or of the becoming
of a character.

The *historical* configuration is one of relationships between
the action of Part One and its recall in Part Two, and
between the success of Part One in the historical world of
1605-1614, and its effect on Cervantes' delineation of his
characters in the sequel. At the beginning of Part One in 1605
the hidalgo is depicted as having lived in the recent past.
Although the story's duration is relatively brief, the account
of his adventures in the form of a history (by the sage Cide
Hamete and his interpreter) is brought forward across the
years onto the stage of the historical world of 1614 (i.e.,
the expulsion of the Moriscos, civil strife in Catalonia).

The *magical* and *prophetical* are confined initially to the
deranged imagination of Don Quijote, but subsequently and
by degrees they pervade the entire course of the story
and direct its movement as fiction (i.e., the fame of Don
Quijote, the enchantment of Dulcinea). The pretext for their
insertion in an exemplary story is initially the parody and
satire of chivalric stories. And subsequently their temporality
is shaped by the power and structure of illusions, in Don
Quijote, in Sancho. The scale of *magical* time unfolds with
the theme of enchantments introduced in Part One to the
feats of deliverance performed by the mock hero in Part
Two. The temporality of Don Quijote's fame is borne forward
and beyond the confines of his book by the scale of *prophetic*
time. In a sense, this *prophetic* time is renewed and fulfilled
in each of Cervantes' readers who recreates for himself Don
Quijote's illusion and his triumph over ridicule and disbelief.

Too much perhaps has already been said about the
mythical configuration. Yet I cannot forego a final remark
that may serve as a threshold to a more definitive study on
temporal elements in Cervantes' novel. The detailed critical

study of what we know as the process of invention (or composition, elaboration, etc., i.e., la *invención* del *Quijote*) will show, I believe, that the end and means of that process from Part One through Part Two was the continuous enlargement and elaboration of his exemplary story within a mythical figuration for his hero. So long as we lacked the proper perspective onto the temporal movement of the story the true magnitude of that process as the outward unfolding of his fiction to its consummate form and meaning would necessarily evade us. Not the incident, but the force with which temporal configuration in *Don Quijote* reveals the permanence of this book should be cause for amazement, for it tells us in the way a story should that the 'nuclear' structure of a literary work is myth.

NOTES TO CHAPTER IV

1. I have depended heavily on the studies of R. S. Loomis. On elements of solar mythology in Lancelot and his legend see *Celtic Myth and Arthurian Romance* (Columbia Univ. Press, 1927), Ch. 9. Hereafter I refer to this study with the abbreviation *CMAR*, and to the following, also by Loomis, and with an abbreviation: *Arthurian Tradition and Chrétien de Troyes* (Columbia Univ. Press, 1949), abbreviation: *ATCT*. *Wales and the Arthurian Legend* (Cardiff: Univ. of Wales Press, 1956), abbreviation: *WAL*. *The Grail from Celtic Myth to Christian Symbol* (Columbia Univ. Press, 1963), referred to as *Grail*. See also: Hugo Moser, "Mythos und Epos in der hochmittelalterlichen deutschen Dichtung," *Wirkendes Wort*, 15: 145-157 (1965).

2. Loomis, *CMAR*, p. 63.

3. Loomis, *CMAR*, pp. 286-287. On the medieval Christian calendar and liturgical year and their relationships to pagan seasonal festivals see E. O. James, *Seasonal Feasts and Festivals* (London: Thames and Hudson; New York: Barnes & Noble, 1961), Ch. 7, and bibliography, pp. 326-327. To my knowledge Loomis' studies include the most complete discussion available on the importance and influence of Celtic solar mythology on the chivalric (Arthurian) romances. I have found it indispensable to keep theoretical questions of relationships between solar myths, folklore, and anthropology within a purely historical perspective, such as provided by Richard M. Dorson in *The British Folklorists* (London: Routledge & Kegan Paul, 1968), especially Chs. 6 and 7.

4. Loomis, *WAL*, pp. 83-84.

5. Loomis, *WAL*, pp. 81-83.

6. Loomis, *WAL*, p. 85.

7. Loomis, *WAL*, p. 86.

8. See Loomis, *ATCT*, p. 199, and William A. Nitze, "Yvain and the Myth of the Fountain," *Speculum*, 30: 170-179 (1955). The mythical attributes of Chrétien's heroes and what I call the temporal configuration of his romances have been noted by Philippe Ménard, "Le temps et la durée dans les romans de Chrétien de Troyes," *Moyen Age*, 73: 375-401 (1967); see p. 382.

9. As far as I know no adequate study of this chivalric topic or theme exists. At least one of its elements is traceable to Celtic tradition, either through the Merlin legend (on Merlin's madness see A. O. H. Jarman, *The Legend of Merlin* [Univ. of Wales Press, 1960], pp. 12-17) or *The Sickbed of Cuchulainn* (Loomis, *ATCT*, p. 309). The 'wild' and 'crazed man' of Celtic myth and legend is the earliest antecedent and source of Yvain's madness; but its combination with themes and doctrines of *amour courtois* is the decisive factor for chivalric romance and is owed, also, to Chrétien. (However, see J. D. Bruce, *The Evolution of Arthurian Romance*, 2nd ed. [John Hopkins Press, 1928; reprint, Peter Smith, 1958], II, pp. 79-80 note.) In *Yvain* (vs. 2774-3130) the four elements (i.e., their combination) that ultimately appear in *Amadís de Gaula*, transformed by way of the legends of Lancelot and Tristan, are clearly discernible. They can be analyzed according to the following order:

(1) The displeasure and ire of the lady (Laudine, Oriana) are aroused by the knight's actions (Yvain is guilty of negligence, Amadís is innocent, the victim of false reports). In the Lancelot story it is Guenievre's jealousy and ire that are aroused by what she believes to be Lancelot's unfaithfulness (see below). In prose versions of the Tristan story the lady's behavior (Iseult) arouses the knight's jealousy. The *feigned* madness of Tristan in some versions *(La Folie Tristan)* is a separate and different theme, see G. L. van Roosbroeck *Romanic Review*, 26: 45-46 (1935).

(2) Out of grief and remorse the knight loses (or nearly loses) his mind, considering himself completely at fault (Yvain, Lancelot, Amadís, Don Quijote). This second element is related to the so-called "lovers' malady of heroes," see J. L. Lowes, *MPh*, 11: 1-56 (1914). In the Tristan story, specifically *La Tavola Ritonda o l'istoria di Tristano*, ed. F. L. Polidori, sects, LXX ff., and *Le roman en prose de Tristan*, analyse par E. Löseth (Paris, 1890), sects. 76, 101-103, the most direct antecedent for Orlando's madness *(Furioso,* c. 23-24), the knight is crazed by jealousy. See Pio Rajna, *Le fonti dell' "Orlando Furioso*," 2nd. ed. (Firenze, 1900), Ch. 13, pp. 393-408; Giulio Bertoni, *L'"Orlando furioso" e la Rinascenza a Ferrara* (Modena, 1919), pp. 104-107; E. G. Gardner, *The Arthurian Legend in Italian Literature* (London, New York, 1930), pp. 283-284.

(3) In his madness the knight reverts to a 'wild state,' and lives in a forest or wilderness (*Yvain*, vss. 2827-28, "Et tant conversa el boschage / Come hon forsené et sauvage . . ."), and is aided by a hermit

(Yvain, Lancelot, Amadís). It is this element that is related to the legend of the hairy anchorite or penitent and the wild man, see Richard Bernheimer, *Wild Men in the Middle Ages* (New York: Octagon Books, 1970; reprint of Harvard Univ. Press, 1952), pp. 14-15 et passim. In just what way the interweaving of these two legends, and the landscape they evoked, made possible their elaboration (and subordination) within the artistic ends of *amour courtois* has yet to be determined.

(4) The knight undergoes a "spiritual" trial or purgation (suggested in Yvain, explicit in Amadís, gratuitous in Don Quijote) and eventually recovers, and (by the intervention of benevolent dames or damsels) is restored to his lady's favor (Yvain, Amadís). The principal element lacking in the prose *Lancelot* and contained in the *Amadís* is the penitence of the lover-knight, and with it the figure of the hermit as a spiritual guide. That Lancelot in the *Vulgate* versions undergoes three different periods of madness and a subsequent cure is well known (e.g., Bernheimer, loc. cit., and notes). But that Lancelot among the Arthurian heroes is the one knight most particularly prone to aberrant, irrational and neurotic behavior has perhaps not been taken into account sufficiently in the appraisals of his legend as an antecedent to Don Quijote's madness. On the similarities between the Lancelot legend and the *Amadís* see María Rosa Lida de Malkiel in *Arthurian Literature in the Middle Ages, A Collaborative History*, ed. R. S. Loomis (Oxford: Clarendon Press, 1959), pp. 414-415.

The first period of madness for Lancelot follows his imprisonment by the Saxon enchantress Camille, and he is cured by the Damsel of the Lake, *Le Livre de Lancelot del Lac, The Vulgate Version of the Arthurian Romances*, ed. H. Oskar Sommer, 3 vols. ([Washington: Carnegie Institution, 1910-1912], reprint, New York: AMS Press, 1969), I, pp. 414-417. In the second instance, unable to find Galehot, Lancelot falls into a prolonged depression. In his distraught state he roams about the whole summer and winter; on Christmas Eve the Damsel of the Lake finds him in a forest in Cornwall, keeps him in her company, and cures him with an ointment, and by Easter he has recovered his former strength. On Ascension Day he appears at Camaalot, and thereon ensues the train of events that leads to the Queen's abduction by Meleagant and her subsequent rescue by Lancelot, II, pp. 154 ff. The third occasion is quite certainly the direct antecedent for the Beltenebrós episode in the Amadís. At Camaalot, deceived by Brisane for a second time, Lancelot has slept with Helaine, when he thought he was with the Queen. Grieved and incensed by what she considers his unfaithfulness and treachery, Guenievre banishes him from her presence forever. He is unable to speak a word in his defense, and rushes away and goes into the loneliest part of the forest. The occasion at Camaalot has been the feast of Whitsun (Pentecost). Lancelot's companions undertake to look for him; as in the *Amadís* they separate, arranging to meet on Saint John's Day. They fail in their search, for Lancelot, having lost his reason and memory, has wandered aimlessly and has become unrecognizable. This period of madness lasts for more than four years (see F. Lot [cited note 16 below], p. 60), and his 'wild' and demented state brings him to a strange series of adventures. On one occasion he is found by a hermit, who with the help of others takes him to a hermitage and affects a partial cure. Lancelot is eventually healed at Corbenic by the Holy Grail, III, pp. 379 ff.; see Loomis, *Grail,* p. 163.

10. See Loomis, *ATCT,* pp. 312-317. On the motif and literary tradition of the grateful lion in Castilian literature see Miguel Garci-Gómez (who, however, is unaware of some materials covered by Loomis and his references), "La tradición del león reverente: glosas para los episodios en *Mío Cid, Palmerín de Oliva, Don Quijote,* y otros," *Kentucky Romance Quarterly,* 19: 255-284 (1972).

11. See Wm. J. Entwistle, *The Arthurian Legend in the Literature of the Spanish Peninsula* (London: J. M. Dent & Sons, 1925), p. 214, 251-252.

12. See T. P. Cross & Wm. A. Nitze, *Lancelot and Guenevere* (Univ. Chicago Press, 1930).

13. Ibid., pp. 65-66.

14. Loomis, *WAL,* p. 111; *ATCT,* pp. 265-266. See also Ernst Soudek, "Structure and Time in *Le Chevalier de la Charrette,*" *Romania,* 93: 96-108 (1972).

15. *Lancelot,* ed. Sommer, III, p. 381.

16. See the chronology worked out by Ferdinand Lot for the prose Lancelot: *Étude sur le Lancelot en prose* (Paris: Honoré Champion, 1918), Ch. 3; esp. pp. 59-61.

17. The most important classical antecedents for Cervantes appear to be Ovid, *Meta.,* I, vss. 89-112; Seneca, *Epistulae Morales,* n. 90; of the Italians, Tasso, *Aminta,* Act 1, ii; and in Spain, Antonio de Guevara, *Marco Aurelio con el Reloj de príncipes,* Sevilla: Juan Cromberger, 1537, Bk. I, Ch. 31. The extent to which the entire conception of 'golden age: virtue / iron age : depravity' in *Don Quijote* is derived from Guevara is not generally appreciated. On the 'golden age' consult the following: A. Bartlett Giamatti, *The Earthly Paradise and the Renaissance Epic* (Princeton Univ. Press, 1966), pp. 11-33; Harry Levin, *The Myth of the Golden Age in the Renaissance* (Indiana Univ. Press, 1969); and Gustavo Costa, *La leggenda dei Secoli d'Oro nella letteratura italiana* (Bari: Laterza, 1972).

18. Cf. Levin, *Golden Age,* pp. 140-143; Peter N. Dunn, "Two Classical Myths in *Don Quijote,*" *Renaissance and Reformation,* 9: 2-10 (1972).

19. His assumed name in Montalvo's text is *"Beltenebrós,"* given to him by the hermit Andalod. "Yo vos quiero poner vn nombre que será conforme a vuestra persona y angustia en que soys puesto, que vos soys mancebo y muy hermoso y vuestra vida está en grande amargura y en tinieblas; quiero que hayáys nombre Beltenebrós," Bk. II, Ch. 48, p. 396a. By the close of the sixteenth century it was common to pronounce *"Beltenebros,"* with the accent on the penultimate syllable, Rodríguez Marín, *DQ* [I. 15], I, p. 415.

20. Barbara Matulka linked the Beltenebrós episode in the *Amadís* to some versions of the medieval legend of the hairy anchorite and discussed its possible parallels to the novel of Juan de Flores *Grimalte*

y Gradissa (the figure of Pamphilo), *The Novels of Juan de Flores and their European Diffusion* (New York: Institute of French Studies, 1931), pp. 287-294. She also discussed the possible influence of *Grimalte y Gradissa* on the Cardenio episode, and reached a negative conclusion, pp. 311-315. Alan D. Deyermond has noted some analogies between the Beltenebrós episode and the wild man legends, but omitting any mention of their relation to the theme of love madness in the *matière de Bretagne*, "El hombre salvaje en la novela sentimental," *Filología*, 10: 97-111 (1964). Neither of these scholars cared to stress that various strands of these two legends — 'the religious penitent in a wilderness' and 'the wild man' — had come together in chivalric romance (in the *Yvain*) and that the line from Yvain to Tristan and Lancelot leads to Amadís (and Orlando) and to Don Quijote. A similar lack of focus is apparent to me in Pamela Waley's introductory comments (pp. xlii-xliii) to her ed. of *Grimalte y Gradissa* (London: Tamesis Books, 1971). A dissertation by Oleh Mazur, "The Wild Man in the Spanish Renaissance and Golden Age Theater" (Univ. of Pennsylvania, 1966), see pp. 31, 35-37, misconceives the relation of wild man legends to the theme of love madness in chivalric romance. Bernheimer noted the appearance of other wild men *(salvajes)* in *Don Quijote*, II. 20, II. 41, but failed to see that Cervantes' hero assumes the role of 'wild man' and 'hairy penitent' by imitating a love madness that calls for his reversion to a wild state. Don Quijote stripped of his outer clothing, and exposing his hairy members, as he frisks and leaps before Sancho, is the eventual mutation of the wild state and fury of mad knights and lovers. Don Quijote tearing his shirt and tying its shreds into knots and reciting the rosary is the eventual allusion to the legends of religious penitents in the wilderness, from which the versions of penitent lovers in *Amadís de Gaula* and the sentimental novel were elaborated. My comments on these matters here are necessarily general and sketchy, for the topic demands a very detailed study, particularly on the process of an interweaving and transformation of various strands of legend and incidence in chivalric and sentimental romance, from Chrétien de Troyes to Cervantes, a study I must reserve for the future. On the wild man legend and decorative themes, in Spain, see also: Harold V. Livermore, "El caballero salvaje, ensayo de identificación de un juglar," *Revista de Filología Española*, 34: 166-183 (1950); José María Azcárate, "El tema iconográfico del salvaje," *Archivo Español de Arte*, 21: 81-99 (1948).

21. Montalvo's episode was variously imitated in later Spanish prose romances: *Lisuarte de Grecia* (the seventh book of the *Amadís* series) by Feliciano de Silva, in *Florambel de Lucea*, and in *Espejo de Principes y Caualleros*, the cases of the knights Caballero del Febo and Rosicler. See Clemencín [I. 25] II, pp. 288-290. The love madness of these knights is confined to a severe neurosis of much weeping and sighing. Their cases resemble more nearly the courtly treatment of jealousy, despair and misunderstanding among lovers in the sentimental novel than the madness of Lancelot, Tristan in the *Tavola Ritonda*, or Orlando. To my knowledge, the episode of Tristan's jealousy as told in the *Tavola Ritonda* did not form part of the Spanish versions of the Tristan story (see Clemencín's note cited above). In the prose

version *Tristán de Leonís* (Valladolid, 1501), when Tristan and Yseo are separated (she is held a prisoner in a tower by King Mares), Brangel is unable to come to his aid and cure him of a poisonous wound, but she advises him to seek help abroad in Brittany (ed. Bonilla y San Martín, Madrid, 1912, Chs. 37-38). When Yseo learns that Tristan has married "Yseo de las blancas manos" she sends a letter to him with Brangel, complaining of his infidelity (Chs. 41-42). On reading it, Tristan is overcome with grief and falls from his horse in a death-like swoon. This is the only trace of love madness that in the case of Amadís is fully described (see Bonilla's Introd., pp. XLVIII-XLIX). The "cauallero saluaje" named Dinadan that we find in this work (Ch. 54) is a type of the comical and non-conforming knight in love and combat. See R. Menéndez Pidal, *Poesía juglaresca* (Madrid: Instituto de Estudios Políticos, 1957), 6th ed., pp. 24-27.

22.   The case of Cardenio, and Don Quijote's imitation of him, is discussed by Edward Dudley in the vol. edited by him and Maximillian E. Novak, *The Wild Man Within* (Univ. of Pittsburgh Press, 1972), "The Wild Man Goes Baroque," pp. 115-139. Dudley follows the line of discussion of previous studies on the figure of the wild man in the sentimental novel to his psycho-moralistic thesis of the Baroque hero. Surprisingly, he fails to see that Don Quijote is likewise inscribed within the convention of chivalresque love madness and the wild man. An important omission in Dudley's accounting of literary antecedents is the figure of the sorrowing knight in the *Romancero*. Menéndez Pidal, *Un aspecto*, pp. 50-51, noted the influence on Cervantes (specifically in I. 23) of a ballad by Juan del Encina, *Cancionero* (Salamanca, 1496; facsimile, Madrid, 1928), f. 87; Durán, n. 1420. On *Orlando* as an antecedent for Cardenio's madness, see Maxime Chevalier, *L'Arioste en Espagne* (Bordeaux, 1966), p. 459.

23.   Don Quijote's performance is not the exact imitation of any of his literary models, Amadís, Orlando, Cardenio, etc. He improvises according to his own conception: he must be 'mad' — *loco* —, abandon himself to the wilds in solitude, strip off his clothing, and perform 'furies'; he must be the penitent, pray, and compose verses, etc. As a matter of accuracy, one cannot say that Amadís de Gaula goes mad or insane (a fact Don Quijote admits in a moment of great lucidity) but the question here is that our hidalgo sees Beltenebrós as 'the mad knight,' 'the wild man,' and 'grieving penitent of love.' The pranks to be done while stripped of his clothes are due to the effect produced by Cardenio in I. 23. On Don Quijote's imitations as artistic see Edward C. Riley, "Don Quixote and the Imitation of Models," *Bulletin of Hispanic Studies*, 31: 3-16 (1954).

24.   Dapple's disappearance (theft) is explicable as a circumstance leading to Don Quijote's isolation and solitude. It was not an afterthought on the part of Cervantes.

25.   Cf. the dialogue between Amadís and Gandalín, Bk. II, Ch. 48, p. 392.

26.   See my article, "The Summer of Myth," pp. 154-155.

27.   See Ch. 2, p. 53 and note 16.

28. Cf. Terrero, "Las rutas," p. 30.

29. On the temporal elements of the cave adventure: Harry Sieber, "Literary Time in the 'Cueva de Montesinos,'" *Modern Language Notes*, 83: 268-273 (1971); María Rosa Lida de Malkiel, on the cave as a vision of the otherworld, in H. R. Patch, *El otro mundo en la literatura medieval* (México: Fondo de Cultura Económica, 1956), Apéndice, "La visión de trasmundo en las literaturas hispánicas," pp. 422-426. On the passage of time in medieval tales of the underworld see Patch's Chs. 1-3. On Cervantes and classical antecedents of the descent of the hero to the underworld see Marasso, op. cit., pp. 141-142, 147-150; Dunn, op. cit., pp. 6-8.

30. Don Quijote's question casts doubts on whether a heart could really be 'extracted' in this way. The detail evidently fascinated Cervantes because he has Durandarte reply ambiguously: "ya con puñal, ya con daga," i.e., "with one or the other." The commentators of *Don Quijote* (see Rodríguez Marín, II. 23) usually cite the ballad "Por el rastro de la sangre" from Lucas Rodríguez *Romancero historiado* (1582) as the source for Cervantes' verses in the episode. But the verses that Cervantes had in mind belong to another version of the same ballad, as preserved in Damián López de Tortajada, *Floresta de varios romances* (Valencia, 1652). Cf. the texts ed. by Antonio Rodríguez-Moñino (Madrid: Castalia, 1967 and 1970). Clemencín's note quotes the version from the *Floresta*, but his editors failed to supply the reference. Now, the earliest known version of these verses appears in 1652 (see Rodríguez-Moñino's Introd. to the *Floresta*). It is not impossible, therefore, that Don Quijote's question and Durandarte's reply are the source, rather than the consequence, of these verses in the ballad: "Lo que os encomiendo primo / . . . Me saqueis el coraçon / con esta pequeña daga. . . ."

31. See the significant essay by Mariano Ibérico Rodríguez, "El Retablo de Maese Pedro, estudio sobre el sentimiento del tiempo en Don Quijote," *Letras* (Lima), n. 54-55: 5-23 (1955).

32. On the figure of the dueña see the important diss. by Conchita Herman Marianella, "A Study of the 'Doña Rodríguez' Episode . . . as part of the larger theme of 'dueñas y doncellas' [i.e., 'dames et damoisels']," Univ. of California, Berkeley, 1973.

33. On Roque Guinart see Martín de Riquer, *Aproximación al "Quijote"* (Barcelona: Teide, 1967), pp. 158-162; Lorenzo Riber, "Al margen de un capítulo [II. 60] de *Don Quijote*," *Boletín de la Real Academia Española*, 27: 79-90 (1947-48). On Ricote and moriscos see: Vicente Lloréns, "Historia y ficción en el *Quijote*," *Literatura, historia, política* (Madrid: Revista de Occidente, 1967), pp. 143-165.

34. A prime example: in the *Vulgate* version of the Lancelot story the Damsel of the Lake decides that the boy will be dubbed by King Arthur on the feastday of Saint John, and so brings it about, *Lancelot*, ed. Sommer, I, pp. 118 ff. The sources of information on folk customs and beliefs related to celebrations at Midsummer (e.g., *The Golden Bough*), and the references to them, are well known. Consult Schevill-Bonilla, eds. *Comedias y entremeses*, III, note p. 247; Loomis, *ATCT*, p. 94, note. On Saint John's Day in Spanish chivalric

romances see Clemencín's Comentario, *DQ* [II. 62], VI, pp. 259-263; Juan Givanel Mas, in Cortejón's ed., *DQ* [II. 61], VI, pp. 249-254 note; also my article, "The Summer of Myth."

35.   "The Christ of fiction," to my knowledge, was first applied to Don Quijote by G. E. Morrison in the Preface to his play, *Alonzo Quixano, Otherwise Don Quixote* (London: Elkin Mathews [1895?]), p. 15.

BIBLIOGRAPHY

1. References to Cervantes' works:

COMPLETE WORKS

Obras completas de Miguel de Cervantes Saavedra, ed. Rodolfo Schevill and Adolfo Bonilla. Madrid: Imp. de Bernardo Rodríguez; Gráficas Reunidas; 1914-1941. 18 vols. Referred to as S-B.
Novelas ejemplares. 3 vols.
Comedias y Entremeses. 6 vols.
Don Quixote de la Mancha. 4 vols. 1928-1941.

OTHER EDITIONS OF "DON QUIJOTE"

Historia del famoso cavallero Don Quixote de la Mancha, ed. John Bowle. London and Salisbury, 1781. 6 vols. (in 3).

El ingenioso hidalgo Don Quixote de la Mancha.... Nueva edición, etc., por Juan Antonio Pellicer. Madrid: Gabriel de Sancha. 5 vols. 1-3, 1797; 4-5, 1798.

El ingenioso hidalgo Don Quijote de la Mancha, comentado por Diego Clemencín. Madrid: D. E. Aguado, 1833-1839. 6 vols.

El ingenioso hidalgo Don Quijote de la Mancha.... Edición, etc., por J[uan]. E[ugenio]. Hartzenbusch. Argamasilla de Alba: Imp. de don Manuel Rivadeneyra (casa que fue prisión de Cervantes), 1863, 4 vols.

El ingenioso hidalgo Don Quijote de la Mancha, ... etc., por Clemente Cortejón; continuada (vol. 6) por Juan Givanel y Mas y Juan Suñé Benajes. Madrid: Victoriano Suárez, 1905-1913. 6 vols.

El ingenioso hidalgo Don Quijote de la Mancha, ed. Francisco Rodríguez Marín. Madrid: Ediciones "Atlas," 1947-1949. 10 vols. Referred to as RM.

Don Quijote de la Mancha, seguido del "Quijote" de Avellaneda, ed. Martín de Riquer. Clásicos Planeta: *Obras completas de Miguel de Cervantes.* Barcelona, 1968. 3rd ed.

El ingenioso hidalgo Don Quijote de la Mancha, ed. Luis Andrés Murillo, Madrid: Editorial Castalia (publication forthcoming). 3 vols. Vol. 3 contains the *Bibliografía Fundamental.*

This listing is restricted to the items that have to do specifically with temporal elements in *Don Quijote.* Since in my forthcoming edition I include an extensive bibliography for the entire contents of the book and the criticism on it, in many cases chapter by chapter, I have not wished to duplicate it here even partially.

2. On 'chronology', listed by date of publication. I am listing all the proposals known to me in the hope that this information will serve to discourage further attempts on an overworked topic:

Ríos, Vicente [Diego Gutiérrez] de los, "Plan cronológico del *Quijote*," in *Juicio crítico o análisis del "Quijote*," v. 1 of ed. publ. by Real Academia Española, Madrid, 1780.

Pellicer, Juan Antonio, "Discurso preliminar," v. 1 of his ed., Madrid, 1797, pp. xxv-xxxii.

Eximeno [y Pujades], Antonio, *Apología de Miguel de Cervantes sobre los yerros que se le han notado en el "Quixote*." Madrid: Imp. de la Administración del Real Arbitrio, 1806.

Clemencín, Diego, "Comentario": ed. Madrid, 1833-1839.

Hartzenbusch, Juan Eugenio, "Diario para la mejor inteligencia de los viajes y aventuras de don Quijote," v. 1, pp. xlv-lv, ed. Argamasilla de Alba, 1863. Also, vol. 4 (note 96, Ch. 61), pp. 346-347.

Givanel y Mas, Juan, "Notes," ed. Cortejón, vol. 6 (1913), Ch. 61, pp. 249-255, Ch. 65, pp. 360-365.

Ramboz, Ina W., "Una investigación del plan cronológico y geográfico de *El ingenioso hidalgo* ..." Thesis, M.A., University of Southern California, 1930.

Peralta y Maroto, Rafael, *Cosas del "Quijote*." *Comentarios y artículos* ... Madrid: 1944. "Cronología (1931)," pp. 9-37.

Dale, George Irving, "The Chronology of *Don Quijote*, Part I," *Hispania*, 21: 179-186 (1938).

Sánchez Pérez, J. B., *El ingenioso hidalgo don Quijote de la Mancha. Ruta y cronología.* Madrid-Cádiz: Escelicer, 1941.

Castro Silva, José Vicente, *Prólogo y epílogo de "Don Quijote*," Bogotá: Antares, 1956. Apéndice: Justificación de la cronología de *Don Quijote*, pp. 161-172.

Agostini Banus, Edgar R., *Breve estudio del tiempo y del espacio en el "Quijote*." Ciudad Real: Publicaciones del Instituto de Estudios Manchegos, C. S. I. C., 1958.

3. On mythical (or mythological) elements:

Dunn, Peter N., "Two Classical Myths in *Don Quijote*," *Renaissance and Reformation*, 9: 2-10 (1972).

Marasso, Arturo, *Cervantes, la invención del "Quijote*," Buenos Aires: Libr. Hachette, 1954.

Murillo, L. A., "The Summer of Myth: *Don Quijote de la Mancha* and *Amadís de Gaula, Philological Quarterly,* 51: 145-157 (1972).

Ibérico Rodríguez, Mariano, "'El retablo de maese Pedro', estudio sobre el sentimiento del tiempo en *Don Quijote,*" *Letras,* n. 54-55: 5-23 (1955).

4. Also:

Buchanan, M[ilton] A., "The works of Cervantes and their dates of composition," *Transactions of the Royal Society of Canada,* 3rd series, sec. ii, v. 32: 23-39 (1938).

Gómez Galán, Antonio, "El día y la noche en el *Quijote,*" *Arbor,* 49, n. 185: 33-43 (May 1961).

Sieber, Harry, "Literary time in the 'Cueva de Montesinos,'" *Modern Language Notes,* 86: 268-273 (1971).

Snodgrass El Saffar, Ruth, "The Function of the Fictional Narrator in *Don Quijote,*" *Modern Language Notes,* 83: 164-177 (1968).

Terrero, José, "Las rutas de las tres salidas de don Quijote...," *Anales cervantinos,* 8: 1-49 (1959-60).

———, "Itinerario del *Quijote* de Avellaneda y su influencia en el cervantino," *Anales cervantinos,* 2: 159-191 (1952).

Urzáis, Eduardo R., "La unidad de tiempo en el *Quijote,*" in *Exégesis cervantina,* Mérida: Ediciones de la Universidad de Yucatán, 1950, pp. 27-38.

Wardropper, Bruce W., "*Don Quixote:* Story or History?" *Modern Philology,* 63: 1-11 (1965).

And brief discussions in the following:

Casalduero, Joaquín, *Sentido y forma de las "Novelas ejemplares,"* Buenos Aires: Instituto de Filología, 1943, pp. 34-36.

Togeby, Knud, *La composition du roman "Don Quijote,"* Supplément de *Orbis Litterarum,* 1967, pp. 7-8.

INDEX

Aestiva regio, 126.

Alba, Duke of, 60, 73.

Alemán, Mateo, 81-82.

Amadís de Gaula, 122, 125, 133-135, *et passim;* and Arthurian tradition, 137; as Beltenebrós, *see* 'Wild man' legend.

Ariosto, *Orlando furioso*, 10, 135-136, 164 n. 9, *et passim*.

Arms and letters, discourse on, 131.

Arthur, King, 119, 124, *et passim*.

Arthurian legend, 119-120, 137, 163-164.

Astrana Marín, Luis, 82, 110 n. 2.

Astrolabe, 40.

Avellaneda, 107, 108-109, 116, 153.

Barcelona, as destination, 24, 26-27, 156-157; *see also* Festivals, Saint John's Day.

Boccaccio, 10.

Bowle, John, 68 n. 4, 8.

Castro, Américo, 81, 111 n. 9.

"Canción de Grisóstomo" ("Desperate Lover's Song"), 77, 85-86, 112 n. 22.

Captain's (Ruy Pérez) story, 72-73; analyzed, 92-98.

Cardenio, 84, 88-89, 132; as 'wild man,' 134.

El celoso extremeño, 72.

Cervantes, Andalusian period, 77, 82; and Captain's story, 73-74, 93-95; his cosmography, 40; petition to Crown in 1590, 73; imprisoned, 76; revises draft of *DQ*, 80, 85, 110 n. 2; and phases of composition, 75, 101, 106, 110.

Chrétien de Troyes, 119, 125; Lancelot *(Le Chevalier de la Charrete)*, 122, and Guenievre, 123, 149; *Yvain*, 118, 121-122, 164 n. 9.

Chronology, 10, 12, 21, 39-42, 56, 63, 74, *et passim*.

Cide Hamete, 33-34, 100, 158, *et passim*.

Clemencín, Diego, 42, 56, *et passim*.

Clocks, 40, 68 n. 5.

El curioso impertinente, 75, 90, 91-92, 98.

Damsels, 120, 130, 165 n. 9; *see also* 'Dueñas y doncellas.'

Dapple, theft of, 135, 168 n. 24.

Dates, 48, 56-57, 88; in Captain's story, 73, 75.

175